Presented to

_____

By

_____

Date

_____

Armed
AND
Dangerous

Armed
AND
Dangerous

AMPED EDITION

EPHESIANS 6:11
STRAIGHT
ANSWERS
FROM THE
BIBLE

BARBOUR
PUBLISHING

Published by Barbour Publishing, Inc., P.O. Box 719, Uhrichsville, Ohio 44683, www.barbourbooks.com

Our mission is to publish and distribute inspirational products offering exceptional value and biblical encouragement to the masses.

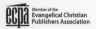
Member of the
Evangelical Christian
Publishers Association

Printed in the United States of America.

Contents

Introduction

Most of us have spent a lot of time flipping through the pages of the Bible, looking for what God's Word says about a certain subject. It's frustrating when you can't find the information you are looking for: "I know the Bible talks about this issue someplace; I just can't figure out where!" Many students get discouraged and give up the search without satisfaction.

For more than twenty years, *Armed and Dangerous* has been the antidote for that frustration. Many key verses of scripture that relate to the compelling issues of our time—topics such as Accountability, Drug Abuse, Hypocrisy, Peer Pressure, Thoughts, and many more—are contained in this one compact volume. And now, each of the topics—more than one hundred in all—is accompanied by quotations, facts, definitions, and other helpful information.

Because the scriptures are arranged topically, you can use *Armed and Dangerous* as a study guide, reference resource, or devotional aid in your own walk with God.

When you need straight answers—straight from the Bible—turn to *Armed and Dangerous*, God's Word for your contemporary condition.

Abortion

Def.: the termination of a pregnancy after, accompanied by, resulting in, or closely followed by the death of the embryo or fetus: induced expulsion of a human fetus.

# of U.S. abortions in 2007: 1.2 million
% of pregnancies ending in abortion: 22

And God said, Let us make man in our image, after our likeness.

GENESIS 1:26

I praise you because I am fearfully and wonderfully made; your works are wonderful, I know that full well. My frame was not hidden from you when I was made in the secret place, when I was woven together in the depths of the earth. Your eyes saw my unformed body; all the days ordained for me were written in your book before one of them came to be.

PSALM 139:14–16 NIV

Can a woman forget her sucking child, that she should not have compassion on the son of her womb? yea, they may forget, yet will I not forget thee.

ISAIAH 49:15

Before I formed thee in the belly I knew thee; and before thou camest forth out of the womb I sanctified thee, and I ordained thee a prophet unto the nations.

JEREMIAH 1:5

Children are an heritage of the LORD: and the fruit of the womb is his reward.

PSALM 127:3

Thou shalt not kill.

EXODUS 20:13; DEUTERONOMY 5:17

There is a way that seemeth right unto a man, but the end thereof are the ways of death.

PROVERBS 16:25

And it came to pass, that, when Elisabeth heard the salutation of Mary, the babe leaped in her womb; and Elisabeth was filled with the Holy Ghost.

LUKE 1:41

But when it pleased God, who separated me from my mother's womb, and called me by his grace. . .

GALATIANS 1:15

Forgiveness for aborting a baby

Wash you, make you clean; put away the evil of your doings from before mine eyes; cease to do evil; Learn to do well; seek judgment, relieve the oppressed, judge the fatherless, plead for the widow. Come now, and let us reason together, saith the LORD: though your sins be as scarlet, they shall be as white as snow; though they be red like crimson, they shall be as wool.

ISAIAH 1:16–18

If we confess our sins, he is faithful and just to forgive us our sins, and to cleanse us from all unrighteousness.

1 JOHN 1:9

Let the wicked forsake his way, and the unrighteous man his thoughts: and let him return unto the LORD, and he will have mercy upon him; and to our God, for he will abundantly pardon.

ISAIAH 55:7

But if we walk in the light, as he is in the light, we have fellowship one with another, and the blood of Jesus Christ his Son cleanseth us from all sin.

1 JOHN 1:7

And Jesus said unto her, Neither do I condemn thee: go, and sin no more.

JOHN 8:11

Q: Even some who support abortion rights have said it should be "rare"—what can you do to help limit the number of abortions?

Abuse

Def.: in teenage relationships, abuse ranges from manipulation, mind-games, and insults (being called stupid, worthless, or ugly), to character assassination, physical violence, or rape.

According to a 2008 survey by Teenage Research Unlimited, one in three teen girls has been a victim of physical, emotional, or verbal abuse from a dating partner.

For the abused person

Come unto me, all ye that labour and are heavy laden, and I will give you rest.

MATTHEW 11:28

I sought the LORD, and he answered me; he delivered me from all my fears. Those who look to him are radiant; their faces are never covered with shame.

PSALM 34:4-5 NIV

Trust ye in the LORD for ever: for in the LORD JEHOVAH is everlasting strength: For he bringeth down them that dwell on high; the lofty city, he layeth it low; he layeth it low, even to the ground; he bringeth it even to the dust.

ISAIAH 26:4–5

Casting all your care upon him; for he careth for you.

1 PETER 5:7

Trust in the LORD with all thine heart; and lean not unto thine own understanding. In all thy ways acknowledge him, and he shall direct thy paths.

PROVERBS 3:5–6

Why, my soul, are you downcast? Why so disturbed within me? Put your hope in God, for I will yet praise him, my Savior and my God.

PSALM 42:11 NIV

For the abusive person

Husbands, love your wives, even as Christ also loved the church, and gave himself for it. . . . So ought men to love their wives as their own bodies. He that loveth his wife loveth himself. For no man ever yet hated his own flesh; but nourisheth and cherisheth it, even as the Lord the church.

EPHESIANS 5:25, 28, 29

Or do you not know that wrongdoers will not inherit the kingdom of God? Do not be deceived: Neither the sexually immoral nor idolaters nor adulterers nor men who have sex with men nor thieves nor the greedy nor drunkards nor slanderers nor swindlers will inherit the kingdom of God. And that is what some of you were. But you were washed, you were sanctified, you were justified in the name of the Lord Jesus Christ and by the Spirit of our God.

1 CORINTHIANS 6:9–11 NIV

But the fruit of the Spirit is love, joy, peace, longsuffering, gentleness, goodness, faith, Meekness, temperance: against such there is no law.

GALATIANS 5:22–23

Likewise, ye husbands, dwell with them according to knowledge, giving honour unto the wife, as unto the weaker vessel, and as being heirs together of the grace of life; that your prayers be not hindered.

1 PETER 3:7

Q: Do you know the difference between relationship problems and abuse? How can you respond effectively to abuse?

Accountability

Def.: Acknowledging and assuming responsibility for actions and decisions, including the obligation to report and explain them, and to be answerable for mistakes and misconduct.

It is easy to dodge our responsibilities, but we cannot dodge the consequences of dodging our responsibilities.

Sir Josiah Stamp

So then every one of us shall give account of himself to God.

Romans 14:12

For we are taking pains to do what is right, not only in the eyes of the Lord but also in the eyes of man.

2 Corinthians 8:21 NIV

For we must all appear before the judgment seat of Christ; that every one may receive the things done in his body, according to that he hath done, whether it be good or bad.

2 Corinthians 5:10

Iron sharpeneth iron; so a man sharpeneth the countenance of his friend.

Proverbs 27:17

But I say unto you, That every idle word that men shall speak, they shall give account thereof in the day of judgment. For by thy words thou shalt be justified, and by thy words thou shalt be condemned.

Matthew 12:36–37

Obey them that have the rule over you, and submit yourselves: for they watch for your souls, as they that must give account, that they may do it with joy, and not with grief: for that is unprofitable for you.

Hebrews 13:17

And he said also unto his disciples, There was a certain rich man, which had a steward; and the same was accused unto him that he had wasted his goods. And he called him, and said unto him, How is it that I hear this of thee? give an account of thy stewardship; for thou mayest be no longer steward.

Luke 16:1–2

"When I say to the wicked, 'You wicked person, you will surely die,' and you do not speak out to dissuade them from their ways, that wicked person will die for their sin, and I will hold you accountable for their blood. But if you do warn the wicked person to turn from their ways and they do not do so, they will die for their sin, though you yourself will be saved."

Ezekiel 33:8–9 NIV

Q: You're accountable to your boss when you have a job, but who are you accountable to spiritually?

Adultery

% of married men who have an extramarital affair: about 60

% of married women who have an extramarital affair: about 40

A little flirtation is harmless but you're dealing with fire here. The fidelity bank and trust is a tough creditor. You make a deposit somewhere else, they close your account—*forever.*

FROM THE MOVIE *THE FAMILY MAN*

Thou shalt not commit adultery.

EXODUS 20:14

"If a man commits adultery with another man's wife—with the wife of his neighbor—both the adulterer and the adulteress are to be put to death."

LEVITICUS 20:10 NIV

But a man who commits adultery has no sense; whoever does so destroys himself.

PROVERBS 6:32 NIV

If a woman shall put away her husband, and be married to another, she committeth adultery.

MARK 10:12

Ye have heard that it was said by them of old time,
Thou shalt not commit adultery: But I say unto you, That
whosoever looketh on a woman to lust after her hath
committed adultery with her already in his heart.

MATTHEW 5:27–28

Whosoever putteth away his wife, and marrieth another,
committeth adultery: and whosoever marrieth her that is
put away from her husband committeth adultery.

LUKE 16:18

Know ye not that the unrighteous shall not inherit the
kingdom of God? Be not deceived: neither fornicators,
nor idolaters, nor adulterers, nor effeminate, nor abusers
of themselves with mankind, nor thieves, nor covetous, nor
drunkards, nor revilers, nor extortioners, shall inherit the
kingdom of God.

1 CORINTHIANS 6:9–10

Marriage is honourable in all, and the bed undefiled: but
whoremongers and adulterers God will judge.

HEBREWS 13:4

For out of the heart proceed evil thoughts, murders,
adulteries, fornications, thefts, false witness, blasphemies. . . .

MATTHEW 15:19

He that covereth his sins shall not prosper: but whoso
confesseth and forsaketh them shall have mercy.

PROVERBS 28:13

If we confess our sins, he is faithful and just to forgive us our sins, and to cleanse us from all unrighteousness.

1 JOHN 1:9

Jesus said unto her, Neither do I condemn thee: go, and sin no more.

JOHN 8:11

Q: What steps can you take right now to make your future marriage adultery-proof?

Alcohol

In the United States:

- Almost one-third of teens have ridden in a car with a drunk teen driver
- About half of teens who commit suicide are under the influence of alcohol

No one thinks he will become a slave to alcohol.

JERRY DUNN
GOD IS FOR THE ALCOHOLIC

Wine is a mocker, strong drink is raging: and whosoever is deceived thereby is not wise.

PROVERBS 20:1

He that loveth wine and oil shall not be rich.

PROVERBS 21:17

Do not join those who drink too much wine or gorge themselves on meat, for drunkards and gluttons become poor, and drowsiness clothes them in rags.

PROVERBS 23:20–21 NIV

Woe unto them that rise up early in the morning, that they may follow strong drink; that continue until night, till wine inflame them!

ISAIAH 5:11

Who hath woe? who hath sorrow? who hath contentions? who hath babbling? who hath wounds without cause? who hath redness of eyes? They that tarry long at the wine; they that go to seek mixed wine.

PROVERBS 23:29–30

"Be careful, or your hearts will be weighed down with carousing, drunkenness and the anxieties of life, and that day will close on you suddenly like a trap."

LUKE 21:34 NIV

Let us walk honestly, as in the day; not in rioting and drunkenness.

ROMANS 13:13

Do you not know that wrongdoers will not inherit the kingdom of God? Do not be deceived: Neither the sexually immoral nor idolaters nor adulterers nor men who have sex with men nor thieves nor the greedy nor drunkards nor slanderers nor swindlers will inherit the kingdom of God.

1 CORINTHIANS 6:9-10 NIV

Envyings, murders, drunkenness, revellings, and such like: of the which I tell you before, as I have also told you in time past, that they which do such things shall not inherit the kingdom of God.

GALATIANS 5:21

And be not drunk with wine, wherein is excess; but be filled with the Spirit.

EPHESIANS 5:18

Therefore if any man be in Christ, he is a new creature: old things are passed away; behold, all things are become new.

2 CORINTHIANS 5:17

I beseech you therefore, brethren, by the mercies of God, that ye present your bodies a living sacrifice, holy, acceptable unto God, which is your reasonable service. And be not conformed to this world: but be ye transformed by the renewing of your mind, that ye may prove what is that good, and acceptable, and perfect, will of God.

ROMANS 12:1–2

If the Son therefore shall make you free, ye shall be free indeed.

JOHN 8:36

Q: What safeguards do you have in place in your life to prevent you from abusing alcohol?

Ambition

Def.: the determination to achieve success or distinction. Godly ambition spurs us to attempt great things; ambition motivated by pride or greed is a vice.

Ambition must be tempered by self-control. It isn't somebody else's job to hold your ambition in check.

MARK ELFSTRAND
10 PASSIONS OF A MAN'S SOUL

Do nothing out of selfish ambition or vain conceit. Rather, in humility value others above yourselves.

PHILIPPIANS 2:3 NIV

For what is a man profited, if he shall gain the whole world, and lose his own soul? or what shall a man give in exchange for his soul?

MATTHEW 16:26

Make it your ambition to lead a quiet life: You should mind your own business and work with your hands, just as we told you, so that your daily life may win the respect of outsiders and so that you will not be dependent on anybody.

1 THESSALONIANS 4:11–12 NIV

For where you have envy and selfish ambition, there you find disorder and every evil practice.

JAMES 3:16 NIV

Q: How can ambition help you to fulfill God's will? How can ambition cause you to miss God's will?

Anger

I know a few techniques that could help you manage that anger very effectively.

FROM *THE INCREDIBLE HULK*

Fools give full vent to their rage, but the wise bring calm in the end.

PROVERBS 29:11 NIV

He that is soon angry dealeth foolishly: and a man of wicked devices is hated.

PROVERBS 14:17

He that is slow to wrath is of great understanding: but he that is hasty of spirit exalteth folly.

PROVERBS 14:29

Cease from anger, and forsake wrath: fret not thyself in any wise to do evil.

PSALM 37:8

A wrathful man stirreth up strife: but he that is slow to anger appeaseth strife.

PROVERBS 15:18

A soft answer turneth away wrath: but grievous words stir up anger.

PROVERBS 15:1

Ye have heard that it was said of them of old time, Thou shalt not kill; and whosoever shall kill shall be in danger of the judgment: But I say unto you, That whosoever is angry with his brother without a cause shall be in danger of the judgment.

MATTHEW 5:21–22

Be ye angry, and sin not: let not the sun go down upon your wrath: Neither give place to the devil.

EPHESIANS 4:26–27

Let all bitterness, and wrath, and anger, and clamour, and evil speaking, be put away from you, with all malice.

EPHESIANS 4:31

Make no friendship with an angry man; and with a furious man thou shalt not go: Lest thou learn his ways, and get a snare to thy soul.

PROVERBS 22:24–25

Q: If you are easily angered, what practical steps can you take to control your temper?

Anxiety

Def.: The National Institute of Mental Health estimates that 40,000,000 Americans suffer from some form of anxiety disorder.

When Christ becomes our central focus, contentment replaces our anxiety as well as our fears and insecurities.

CHARLES R. SWINDOLL
LAUGH AGAIN

Humble yourselves therefore under the mighty hand of God, that he may exalt you in due time: Casting all your care upon him; for he careth for you.

1 PETER 5:6–7

Thou wilt keep him in perfect peace, whose mind is stayed on thee: because he trusteth in thee.

ISAIAH 26:3

Trust in the LORD with all thine heart; and lean not unto thine own understanding. In all thy ways acknowledge him, and he shall direct thy paths.

PROVERBS 3:5–6

But my God shall supply all your need according to his riches in glory by Christ Jesus.

PHILIPPIANS 4:19

Blessed is the man that trusteth in the LORD, and whose hope the LORD is. For he shall be as a tree planted by the waters, and that spreadeth out her roots by the river, and shall not see when heat cometh, but her leaf shall be green; and shall not be careful in the year of drought, neither shall cease from yielding fruit.

JEREMIAH 17:7–8

"Therefore I tell you, do not worry about your life, what you will eat or drink; or about your body, what you will wear. Is not life more important than food, and the body more than clothes? So do not worry, saying, 'What shall we eat?' or 'What shall we drink?' or 'What shall we wear?' But seek first his kingdom and his righteousness, and all these things will be given to you as well. Therefore do not worry about tomorrow, for tomorrow will worry about itself. Each day has enough trouble of its own."

MATTHEW 6:25, 31, 33–34 NIV

Why art thou cast down, O my soul? and why art thou disquieted within me? hope thou in God: for I shall yet praise him, who is the health of my countenance, and my God.

PSALM 42:11

I sought the LORD, and he heard me, and delivered me from all my fears.

PSALM 34:4 NIV

Cast thy burden upon the LORD, and he shall sustain thee: he shall never suffer the righteous to be moved.

PSALM 55:22

Do not be anxious about anything, but in every situation by prayer and petition, with thanksgiving, present your requests to God. And the peace of God, which transcends all understanding, will guard your hearts and your minds in Christ Jesus.

PHILIPPIANS 4:6–7 NIV

And we know that all things work together for good to them that love God, to them who are the called according to his purpose.

ROMANS 8:28

Q: Since prayer and meditation on God's Word reduce anxiety—do you spend enough time doing these?

Appearance

O thou who art gifted with a noble frame, a comely body, boast not thyself therein, for thy gifts come from God.

CHARLES H. SPURGEON

Judge not according to the appearance, but judge righteous judgment.

JOHN 7:24

The LORD seeth not as man seeth; for man looketh on the outward appearance, but the LORD looketh on the heart.

1 SAMUEL 16:7

For we commend not ourselves again unto you, but give you occasion to glory on our behalf, that ye may have somewhat to answer them which glory in appearance, and not in heart.

2 CORINTHIANS 5:12

Your beauty should not come from outward adornment, such as elaborate hairstyles and the wearing of gold jewelry or fine clothes. Rather, it should be that of your inner self, the unfading beauty of a gentle and quiet spirit, which is of great worth in God's sight.

1 PETER 3:3–4 NIV

God does not show favoritism.

GALATIANS 2:6 NIV

Moreover when ye fast, be not, as the hypocrites, of a sad countenance: for they disfigure their faces, that they may appear unto men to fast. Verily I say unto you, They have their reward.

MATTHEW 6:16

Abstain from all appearance of evil.

1 THESSALONIANS 5:22

Q: Are you learning not to judge others based on outward appearances? Can you give them the benefit of the doubt?

Assurance

Def.: The state of certainty; the state of assurance founded upon God's solid, trustworthy promises.

When we receive Christ as our Savior, we receive absolute assurance that we will spend eternity with God. That assurance gives us the hope and the courage to endure sorrow, disappointment, and dangerous, difficult times.

JOEL ROSENBERG
EPICENTER

He that believeth on the Son hath everlasting life: and he that believeth not the Son shall not see life; but the wrath of God abideth on him.

JOHN 3:36

He that hath the Son hath life; and he that hath not the Son of God hath not life. These things have I written unto you that believe on the name of the Son of God; that ye may know that ye have eternal life, and that ye may believe on the name of the Son of God.

1 JOHN 5:12–13

But know that the LORD hath set apart him that is godly for himself: the LORD will hear when I call unto him.

PSALM 4:3

According to the eternal purpose which he purposed in Christ Jesus our Lord: In whom we have boldness and access with confidence by the faith of him. . . .

EPHESIANS 3:11–12

We know that we have passed from death unto life, because we love the brethren. He that loveth not his brother abideth in death.

1 JOHN 3:14

And hereby we know that we are of the truth, and shall assure our hearts before him. For if our heart condemn us, God is greater than our heart, and knoweth all things. Beloved, if our heart condemn us not, then have we confidence toward God.

1 JOHN 3:19–21

Let us draw near with a true heart in full assurance of faith, having our hearts sprinkled from an evil conscience, and our bodies washed with pure water.

HEBREWS 10:22

For I know that my redeemer liveth, and that he shall stand at the latter day upon the earth: And though after my skin worms destroy this body, yet in my flesh shall I see God: Whom I shall see for myself, and mine eyes shall behold, and not another; though my reins be consumed within me.

JOB 19:25–27

The Spirit himself testifies with our spirit that we are God's children.

ROMANS 8:16 NIV

For I am persuaded, that neither death, nor life, nor angels, nor principalities, nor powers, nor things present, nor things to come, nor height, nor depth, nor any other creature, shall be able to separate us from the love of God, which is in Christ Jesus our Lord.

ROMANS 8:38–39

I am not ashamed: for I know whom I have believed, and am persuaded that he is able to keep that which I have committed unto him against that day.

2 TIMOTHY 1:12

Q: Does your certainty that Jesus has saved you depend upon your feelings or upon God's Word?

Astrology

A 2009 Pew Research Center survey shows that

- 25% of the public overall believe in astrology
- 23% of professing Christians believe in astrology

And now it's time for our daily feature: The Astrological Hour. A quick reminder—these reports are not intended to foster belief in astrology, but merely to support people who cannot take responsibility for their own lives.

FROM *THE KENTUCKY FRIED MOVIE*

If there be found among you. . .man or woman, that hath wrought wickedness in the sight of the LORD thy God, in transgressing his covenant, and hath gone and served other gods, and worshipped them, either the sun, or moon, or any of the host of heaven, which I have not commanded. . . Then shalt thou bring forth that man or that woman, which have committed that wicked thing. . . and shalt stone them with stones, till they die.

DEUTERONOMY 17:2–3, 5

Therefore shall evil come upon thee; thou shalt not know from whence it riseth: and mischief shall fall upon thee; thou shalt not be able to put it off: and desolation shall come upon thee suddenly, which thou shalt not know. Stand now with thine enchantments, and with the multitude of thy sorceries, wherein thou hast laboured from thy youth; if so be thou shalt be able to profit, if so be thou mayest prevail. Thou art wearied in the multitude of thy counsels. Let now the astrologers, the stargazers, the monthly prognosticators, stand up, and save thee from these things that shall come upon thee. Behold, they shall be as stubble; the fire shall burn them; they shall not deliver themselves from the power of the flame: there shall not be a coal to warm at, nor fire to sit before it.

ISAIAH 47:11–14

There shall not be found among you any one that maketh his son or his daughter to pass through the fire, or that useth divination, or an observer of times, or an enchanter, or a witch. Or a charmer, or a consulter with familiar spirits, or a wizard, or a necromancer. For all that do these things are an abomination unto the LORD: and because of these abominations the LORD thy God doth drive them out from before thee.

DEUTERONOMY 18:10–12

Thou shalt have no other gods before me. Thou shalt not make unto thee any graven image, or any likeness of any thing that is in heaven above, or that is in the earth beneath, or that is in the water under the earth.

EXODUS 20:3–4

Q: Does the Bible teach that Christianity and astrology are compatible? Which do you trust in?

Attitude

Do you envy people who are able to find something positive in every negative experience? Actually, this isn't just some natural ability. It's learned.

MORT CRIM
GOOD NEWS FOR TOUGH TIMES

Have the same mindset as Christ Jesus.

PHILIPPIANS 2:5 NIV

Therefore, since Christ suffered in his body, arm yourselves also with the same attitude, because whoever suffers in the body is done with sin. As a result, they do not live the rest of their earthly lives for evil human desires, but rather for the will of God.

1 PETER 4:1–2 NIV

You were taught, with regard to your former way of life, to put off your old self, which is being corrupted by its deceitful desires; to be made new in the attitude of your minds; and to put on the new self, created to be like God in true righteousness and holiness.

EPHESIANS 4:22–24 NIV

And herein do I exercise myself, to have always a conscience void to offence toward God, and toward men.

ACTS 24:16

Lie not one to another, seeing that ye have put off the old man with his deeds; And have put on the new man, which is renewed in knowledge after the image of him that created him.

COLOSSIANS 3:9–10

And whatsoever ye do in word or deed, do all in the name of the Lord Jesus, giving thanks to God and the Father by him.

COLOSSIANS 3:17

For the word of God is quick, and powerful, and sharper than any twoedged sword, piercing even to the dividing asunder of soul and spirit. . .and is a discerner of the thoughts and intents of the heart.

HEBREWS 4:12

And let the peace of God rule in your hearts, to the which also ye are called in one body; and be ye thankful.

COLOSSIANS 3:15

Q: What practical, small steps can you take today to give yourself a positive attitude?

Backsliding

Def.: To slide back the way one came; to relapse into worldly ways or attitudes; to fall from a state of virtue into past sins and wrongdoing.

The backslider in heart shall be filled with his own ways. . . .

PROVERBS 14:14

Surely these are poor; they are foolish: for they know not the way of the LORD, nor the judgment of their God. I will get me unto the great men, and will speak unto them; for they have known the way of the LORD, and the judgment of their God: but these have altogether broken the yoke, and burst the bonds. . .because their transgressions are many, and their backslidings are increased.

JEREMIAH 5:4–6

Thou hast forsaken me, saith the LORD, thou art gone backward: therefore will I stretch out my hand against thee, and destroy thee; I am weary with repenting. . .since they return not from their ways.

JEREMIAH 15:6–7

Yea, they turned back and tempted God, and limited the Holy One of Israel.

PSALM 78:41

Nevertheless I have somewhat against thee, because thou hast left thy first love. Remember therefore from whence thou art fallen, and repent, and do the first works; or else I will come unto thee quickly, and will remove thy candlestick out of his place, except thou repent.

REVELATION 2:4-5

They will no longer defile themselves with their idols and vile images or with any of their offenses, for I will save them from all their sinful backsliding, and I will cleanse them. They will be my people, and I will be their God.

EZEKIEL 37:23 NIV

Q: We can backslide in large ways or in small ways. Which areas have you backslidden in?

Bad Habits

Def.: an annoying or harmful practice or way of acting that a person does often, almost without thinking; commonly, a vice that is hard to give up.

Generally, there is one desire or one habit that keeps us from enjoying and tasting the fullness of God.

RAVI ZACHARIAS
"IS THERE NOT A COST?" SERMON

The acts of the flesh are obvious: sexual immorality, impurity and debauchery; idolatry and witchcraft; hatred, discord, jealousy, fits of rage, selfish ambition, dissensions, factions and envy; drunkenness, orgies, and the like. I warn you, as I did before, that those who live like this will not inherit the kingdom of God.

GALATIANS 5:19–21 NIV

He that hath a froward heart findeth no good: and he that hath a perverse tongue falleth into mischief.

PROVERBS 17:20

Thy word have I hid in mine heart, that I might not sin against thee.

PSALM 119:11

The lip of truth shall be established for ever: but a lying tongue is but for a moment. Deceit is in the heart of them that imagine evil: but to the counsellors of peace is joy. Lying lips are abomination to the LORD: but they that deal truly are his delight.

PROVERBS 12:19–20, 22

Live such good lives among the pagans that, though they accuse you of doing wrong, they may see your good deeds and glorify God on the day he visits us.

1 PETER 2:12 NIV

Submit yourselves therefore to God. Resist the devil, and he will flee from you.

JAMES 4:7

Do all things without murmurings and disputings: That ye may be blameless and harmless, the sons of God, without rebuke, in the midst of a crooked and perverse nation, among whom ye shine as lights in the world.

PHILIPPIANS 2:14–15

But shun profane and vain babblings: for they will increase unto more ungodliness.

2 TIMOTHY 2:16

Q: What bad habit do you need to overcome, and do you pray daily for God to help you in this area?

Baptism

Q: The most people baptized at one time in the Bible?

A: About 3,000 (Acts 2:41)

Most of what we do in worldly life is geared toward our staying dry, looking good, not going under. But in baptism. . .you agree to do something that's a little sloppy because at the same time it's also holy, and absurd.

ANNE LAMOTT
TRAVELING MERCIES

In those days came John the Baptist, preaching in the wilderness of Judaea, and saying, Repent ye: for the kingdom of heaven is at hand. I indeed baptize you with water unto repentance. but he that cometh after me is mightier than I, whose shoes I am not worthy to bear: he shall baptize you with the Holy Ghost, and with fire.

MATTHEW 3:1–2, 11

Then cometh Jesus from Galilee to Jordan unto John, to be baptized of him. But John forbad him, saying, I have need to be baptized of thee, and comest thou to me? And Jesus answering said unto him, Suffer it to be so now: for thus it becometh us to fulfil all righteousness. Then he suffered him.

MATTHEW 3:13–15

John answered them, saying, I baptize with water: but there standeth one among you, whom ye know not. . . . The next day John seeth Jesus coming unto him, and saith, Behold the Lamb of God, which taketh away the sin of the world.

JOHN 1:26, 29

Jesus made and baptized more disciples than John, (Though Jesus himself baptized not, but his disciples).

JOHN 4:1–2

Then Peter said unto them, Repent, and be baptized every one of you in the name of Jesus Christ for the remission of sins, and ye shall receive the gift of the Holy Ghost.

ACTS 2:38

Then Ananias went to the house and entered it. Placing his hands on Saul, he said, "Brother Saul, the Lord—Jesus, who appeared to you on the road as you were coming here—has sent me so that you may see again and be filled with the Holy Spirit." Immediately, something like scales fell from Saul's eyes, and he could see again. He got up and was baptized.

ACTS 9:17–18 NIV

There is one body, and one Spirit, even as ye are called in one hope of your calling; One Lord, one faith, one baptism, One God and Father of all, who is above all, and through all, and in you all.

EPHESIANS 4:4–6

"Surely no one can stand in the way of their being baptized with water. They have received the Holy Spirit just as we have."

ACTS 10:47 NIV

At that hour of the night the jailer took them and washed their wounds; then immediately he and all his family were baptized.

ACTS 16:33 NIV

And Crispus, the chief ruler of the synagogue, believed on the Lord with all his house; and many of the Corinthians hearing believed, and were baptized.

ACTS 18:8

Then said Paul, John verily baptized with the baptism of repentance, saying unto the people, that they should believe on him which should come after him, that is, on Christ Jesus. When they heard this, they were baptized in the name of the Lord Jesus.

ACTS 19:4-5

And now why tarriest thou? arise, and be baptized, and wash away thy sins, calling on the name of the Lord.

ACTS 22:16

Know ye not, that so many of us as were baptized into Jesus Christ were baptized into his death? Therefore we are buried with him by baptism into death: that like as Christ was raised up from the dead by the glory of the Father, even so we also should walk in newness of life.

ROMANS 6:3-4

For by one Spirit are we all baptized into one body,
whether we be Jews or Gentiles, whether we be bond or
free; and have been all made to drink into one Spirit.

1 CORINTHIANS 12:13

For ye are all the children of God by faith in Christ Jesus.
For as many of you as have been baptized into Christ have
put on Christ.

GALATIANS 3:26–27

And this water symbolizes baptism that now saves you
also—not the removal of dirt from the body but the pledge
of a clear conscience toward God. It saves you by the
resurrection of Jesus Christ.

1 PETER 3:21 NIV

Q: Have you been baptized? What did it mean
to you? If not, how soon do you plan on taking
this step?

Beauty

Def.: 1. A combination of qualities such as shape, etc., that pleases the senses, especially the sight; 2. a combination of qualities that pleases the intellect or moral sense.

Be assured that God likes what He created you to be, in all your physical features. You are beautiful to Him.

PAT WARREN
WEIGHED BY THE WORD

Charm is deceptive, and beauty is fleeting; but a woman who fears the LORD is to be praised.

PROVERBS 31:30 NIV

As a jewel of gold in a swine's snout, so is a fair woman which is without discretion.

PROVERBS 11:22

A virtuous woman is a crown to her husband: but she that maketh ashamed is as rottenness in his bones.

PROVERBS 12:4

And the name of his wife Abigail: and she was a woman of good understanding, and of a beautiful countenance.

1 SAMUEL 25:3

Your beauty should not come from outward adornment, such as elaborate hairstyles and the wearing of gold jewelry or fine clothes. Rather, it should be that of your inner self, the unfading beauty of a gentle and quiet spirit, which is of great worth in God's sight.

1 PETER 3:3–4 NIV

Rachel was beautiful and well favoured.

GENESIS 29:17

He hath made every thing beautiful in his time.

ECCLESIASTES 3:11

How beautiful upon the mountains are the feet of him that bringeth good tidings, that publisheth peace; that bringeth good tidings of good, that publisheth salvation; that saith unto Zion, Thy God reigneth!

ISAIAH 52:7

Woe unto you, scribes and Pharisees, hypocrites! for ye are like unto whited sepulchres, which indeed appear beautiful outward, but are within full of dead men's bones, and of all uncleanness.

MATTHEW 23:27

And let the beauty of the LORD our God be upon us.

PSALM 90:17

Give unto the LORD the glory due unto his name; worship the LORD in the beauty of holiness.

PSALM 29:2

The glory of young men is their strength: and the beauty of old men is the grey head.

PROVERBS 20:29

Finally, brethren, whatsoever things are true, whatsoever things are honest, whatsoever things are just, whatsoever things are pure, whatsoever things are lovely, whatsoever things are of good report; if there be any virtue, and if there be any praise, think on these things.

PHILIPPIANS 4:8

Q: What things do you find physically beautiful? What actions or qualities do you find spiritually beautiful?

Bitterness

Elizabeth Bennet: Men are either eaten up with arrogance or stupidity. If they are amiable, they are so easily led they have no minds of their own whatsoever.

Mrs. Gardiner: Take care, my love. That savors strongly of bitterness.

FROM THE MOVIE PRIDE AND PREJUDICE

Forgiveness is the key that unlocks the door of resentment and the handcuffs of hate. It is a power that breaks the chains of bitterness and the shackles of selfishness.

WILLIAM ARTHUR WARD

Let all bitterness, and wrath, and anger, and clamour, and evil speaking, be put away from you, with all malice: And be ye kind one to another, tenderhearted, forgiving one another, even as God for Christ's sake hath forgiven you.

EPHESIANS 4:31–32

"Therefore, if you are offering your gift at the altar and there remember that your brother or sister has something against you, leave your gift there in front of the altar. First go and be reconciled to them; then come and offer your gift."

MATTHEW 5:23–24 NIV

Bless those who persecute you; bless and do not curse.

ROMANS 12:14 NIV

Do not repay anyone evil for evil. Be careful to do what is right in the eyes of everyone.

ROMANS 12:17 NIV

Christ also suffered for us, leaving us an example, that ye should follow his steps. . . . Who, when he was reviled, reviled not again; when he suffered, he threatened not; but committed himself to him that judgeth righteously.

1 PETER 2:21, 23

Follow peace with all men, and holiness, without which no man shall see the Lord: Looking diligently lest any man fail of the grace of God; lest any root of bitterness springing up trouble you, and thereby many be defiled.

HEBREWS 12:14–15

Out of the same mouth proceedeth blessing and cursing. My brethren, these things ought not so to be. . . . But if ye have bitter envying and strife in your hearts, glory not, and lie not against the truth. This wisdom descendeth not from above, but is earthly, sensual, devilish.

JAMES 3:10, 14–15

Q: Are you holding a grudge against anyone? Are you refusing to forgive someone who has wronged you?

Born Again (How to Be)

Def.: To be made spiritually alive by God's Holy Spirit entering your life when you trust Jesus to save you; also called "being saved."

86% of teens in church describe themselves as Christian, but only 60% believe that they're saved because of their confession of sin and acceptance of Jesus as Savior.

For God so loved the world, that he gave his only begotten Son, that whosoever believeth in him should not perish, but have everlasting life.

JOHN 3:16

But as many as received him, to them gave he power to become the sons of God, even to them that believe on his name: Which were born, not of blood, nor of the will of the flesh, nor of the will of man, but of God.

JOHN 1:12–13

Jesus answered and said unto him, Verily, verily, I say unto thee, Except a man be born again, he cannot see the kingdom of God.

JOHN 3:3

For all have sinned, and come short of the glory of God.

ROMANS 3:23

That which is born of the flesh is flesh; and that which is born of the Spirit is spirit.

JOHN 3:6

For the wages of sin is death; but the gift of God is eternal life through Jesus Christ our Lord.

ROMANS 6:23

But God, who is rich in mercy, for his great love wherewith he loved us, Even when we were dead in sins, hath quickened us together with Christ. . . . For by grace are ye saved through faith; and that not of yourselves: it is the gift of God: Not of works, lest any man should boast.

EPHESIANS 2:4-5, 8-9

"He himself bore our sins" in his body on the tree, so that we might die to sins and live for righteousness; "by his wounds you have been healed."

1 PETER 2:24 NIV

Very rarely will anyone die for a righteous person, though for a good man someone might possibly dare to die. But God demonstrates his own love for us in this: While we were still sinners, Christ died for us.

ROMANS 5:7-8 NIV

For God sent not his Son into the world to condemn the world; but that the world through him might be saved. He that believeth on him is not condemned: but he that believeth not is condemned already, because he hath not believed in the name of the only begotten Son of God.

JOHN 3:17-18

There is therefore now no condemnation to them which are in Christ Jesus, who walk not after the flesh, but after the Spirit.

ROMANS 8:1

Sirs, what must I do to be saved? And they said, Believe on the Lord Jesus Christ, and thou shalt be saved, and thy house.

ACTS 16:30–31

Moreover, brethren, I declare unto you the gospel which I preached unto you, which also ye have received, and wherein ye stand; By which also ye are saved, if ye keep in memory what I preached unto you, unless ye have believed in vain.

1 CORINTHIANS 15:1–2

For I delivered unto you first of all that which I also received, how that Christ died for our sins according to the scriptures; And that he was buried, and that he rose again the third day according to the scriptures.

1 CORINTHIANS 15:3–4

That if thou shalt confess with thy mouth the Lord Jesus, and shalt believe in thine heart that God hath raised him from the dead, thou shalt be saved. For with the heart man believeth unto righteousness; and with the mouth confession is made unto salvation.

ROMANS 10:9–10

Behold, I stand at the door, and knock: if any man hear my voice, and open the door, I will come in to him, and will sup with him, and he with me.

REVELATION 3:20

For the scripture saith, Whosoever believeth on him shall not be ashamed.

ROMANS 10:11

Seeing ye have purified your souls in obeying the truth through the Spirit unto unfeigned love of the brethren, see that ye love one another with a pure heart fervently: Being born again, not of corruptible seed, but of incorruptible, by the word of God, which liveth and abideth for ever.

1 PETER 1:22–23

Now is the time. . .

If you have never been "born again"—if you have never trusted Jesus Christ as your Savior and invited Him into your life—you can do it right now. If you are not sure you are a Christian, now is the perfect time to make sure. Look back over the preceding scriptures and understand that Jesus died for your sins. He defeated death and the devil; He rose again on the third day; He is now alive and well at the right hand of your heavenly Father. Because He lives, you can live, too—forever with Him in heaven.

Trust in the Lord right now, and ask Him to save you. Pray something similar to this:

Lord Jesus, I know You love me, because You proved it by dying on the cross to pay the penalty for my sins. Thank you, Jesus, for doing that for me.

I admit that I have sinned—against others and against myself, but most of all, against You. Please forgive me for my sins and give me Your power to resist the temptation to sin.

I believe that You rose from the dead and that You really are the only true God. I ask You to come into my life and live at the center of it. Please accept me. By faith, I accept You, Jesus. Thank You for giving me eternal life with You.

If you honestly mean your prayer, Jesus takes you seriously. He causes you to be born again, or you could say, born from above.

This is not the end but rather the beginning of a brand-new way of living. Here are four hints that will help you live for Jesus:

1. *Tell someone what you have done.* It is important to "go on record" that you have been born again. Tell someone who knows you well enough to notice the difference that Jesus will be making in your life. If you have trouble explaining it, just say something like, "I can't explain all the details yet, but I have committed my life to Jesus Christ, and from now on, I'm going to live the way He tells me in His Word."
2. *Begin reading your Bible.* Start with the Gospel of John. Read a bit of the Bible every day.
3. *Pray every day.* Prayer is simply talking to God. He wants to hear from you. Tell Him about your high points, and ask Him to help you through the rough spots.

4. *Go to church regularly.* The church is God's family here on earth. You'll want to be with your church family as frequently as possible for study and service, friendship, and fun.

Q: What determines whether you are a Christian and have truly been born again?

Church

Def.: the Greek word *ekklesia,* commonly translated as "church," actually means "the called-out ones," the congregation or assembly of believers.

According to a 2009 Barna Group survey, Protestant teens aged 13–17 are more likely to go to worship services and attend youth group meetings than were Protestant teens in 1997.

And I say also unto thee, That thou art Peter, and upon this rock I will build my church; and the gates of hell shall not prevail against it.

MATTHEW 16:18

And he is the head of the body, the church: who is the beginning, the firstborn from the dead; that in all things he might have the preeminence.

COLOSSIANS 1:18

Christ is the head of the church: and he is the saviour of the body. Christ also loved the church, and gave himself for it.

EPHESIANS 5:23, 25

For as the body is one, and hath many members, and all the members of that one body, being many, are one body: so also is Christ. For by one Spirit are we all baptized into one body. . .and have been all made to drink into one Spirit. For the body is not one member, but many.

1 CORINTHIANS 12:12–14

Nevertheless the foundation of God standeth sure, having this seal, The Lord knoweth them that are his. And, let every one that nameth the name of Christ depart from iniquity.

2 TIMOTHY 2:19

And they continued stedfastly in the apostles' doctrine and fellowship, and in breaking of bread, and in prayers.

ACTS 2:42

Ye also, as lively stones, are built up a spiritual house, an holy priesthood, to offer up spiritual sacrifices, acceptable to God by Jesus Christ. But ye are a chosen generation, a royal priesthood, an holy nation, a peculiar people; that ye should shew forth the praises of him who hath called you out of darkness into his marvellous light.

1 PETER 2:5, 9

Not giving up meeting together, as some are in the habit of doing, but encouraging one another—and all the more as you see the Day approaching.

HEBREWS 10:25 NIV

Q: Social interaction with Christian teens is important, but how much do you value spiritual fellowship?

Clothes

Natasha Romanoff: They're basically gods.
Steve Rogers: There's only one God, ma'am, and I'm pretty sure He doesn't dress like that.

FROM THE MOVIE *THE AVENGERS*

The beauty of a woman is not in the clothes she wears, the figure that she carries, or the way she combs her hair. The beauty of a woman is seen in her eyes, because that is the doorway to her heart, the place where love resides.

AUDREY HEPBURN

A woman must not wear men's clothing, nor a man wear women's clothing, for the LORD your God detests anyone who does this.

DEUTERONOMY 22:5 NIV

I also want women to dress modestly, with decency and propriety, adorning themselves not with elaborate hairstyles or gold or pearls or expensive clothes, but with good deeds, appropriate for women who profess to worship God.

1 TIMOTHY 2:9–10 NIV

I put on righteousness, and it clothed me: my judgment was as a robe and a diadem.

JOB 29:14

Take no thought for your life, what ye shall eat; neither for the body, what ye shall put on. The life is more than meat, and the body is more than raiment.

LUKE 12:22–23

If you show special attention to the man wearing fine clothes and say, "Here's a good seat for you," but say to the poor man, "You stand there" or "Sit on the floor by my feet," have you not discriminated among yourselves and become judges with evil thoughts?

JAMES 2:3–4 NIV

Beware of false prophets, which come to you in sheep's clothing, but inwardly they are ravening wolves.

MATTHEW 7:15

For we brought nothing into this world, and it is certain we can carry nothing out. And having food and raiment let us be therewith content.

1 TIMOTHY 6:7–8

Q: Do you care too little about your clothes, or too much? How can you strike a proper balance?

Compassion

Def.: Concern for the sorrows and misfortunes of others; pity mixed with empathy that motivates one to be merciful to and to help another.

Helping others means our ears and our eyes are open.

H. NORMAN WRIGHT
HELPING THOSE WHO HURT

Therefore, as God's chosen people, holy and dearly loved, clothe yourselves with compassion, kindness, humility, gentleness and patience.

COLOSSIANS 3:12 NIV

And there shall cleave nought of the cursed thing to thine hand: that the LORD may turn from the fierceness of his anger, and shew thee mercy, and have compassion upon thee, and multiply thee, as he hath sworn unto thy fathers.

DEUTERONOMY 13:17

"This is what the LORD Almighty said: 'Administer true justice; show mercy and compassion to one another. Do not oppress the widow or the fatherless, the foreigner or the poor. Do not plot evil against each other.'"

ZECHARIAH 7:9–10 NIV

Pure religion and undefiled before God and the Father is this, To visit the fatherless and widows in their affliction, and to keep himself unspotted from the world.

JAMES 1:27

He that hath pity upon the poor lendeth unto the LORD; and that which he hath given will he pay him again.

PROVERBS 19:17

A good man sheweth favour, and lendeth: he will guide his affairs with discretion. . . . He hath dispersed, he hath given to the poor; his righteousness endureth for ever; his horn shall be exalted with honour.

PSALM 112:5, 9

Q: Do you merely feel pity for others, or compassion? Does what you feel move you to help others?

Conceit

Obi-Wan: His abilities have made him. . .well, arrogant.
Yoda: Yes. Yes. A flaw more and more common among Jedi. Too sure of themselves they are.

FROM THE MOVIE *STAR WARS: ATTACK OF THE CLONES*

To attempt to advise conceited people is like whistling against the wind.

THOMAS HOOD

Do nothing out of selfish ambition or vain conceit. Rather, in humility value others above yourselves.

PHILIPPIANS 2:3 NIV

The rich man's wealth is his strong city, and as an high wall in his own conceit. Before destruction the heart of man is haughty, and before honour is humility.

PROVERBS 18:11–12

Live in harmony with one another. Do not be proud, but be willing to associate with people of low position. Do not be conceited.

ROMANS 12:16 NIV

Seest thou a man wise in his own conceit? there is more hope of a fool than of him.

PROVERBS 26:12

Pride goeth before destruction, and an haughty spirit before a fall. Better it is to be of an humble spirit with the lowly, than to divide the spoil with the proud.

PROVERBS 16:18–19

Behold, the Lord, the LORD of hosts, shall lop the bough with terror: and the high ones of stature shall be hewn down, and the haughty shall be humbled.

ISAIAH 10:33

Q: Conceit is quite easy to recognize in others, but can you recognize it in yourself?

Confession

Def.: Confess—To acknowledge or admit a sin or fault. Confessing Christ—to openly and publicly declare your faith in Jesus Christ.

Confess to God those sins that have been committed against God, and to man those sins that have been committed against man.

CHARLES FINNEY
LECTURES OF REVIVALS OF RELIGION

I acknowledge my sin unto thee, and mine iniquity have I not hid. I said, I will confess my transgressions unto the LORD; and thou forgavest the iniquity of my sin.

PSALM 32:5

Whoever conceals their sins does not prosper, but the one who confesses and renounces them finds mercy.

PROVERBS 28:13 NIV

Confess your faults one to another, and pray one for another, that ye may be healed. The effectual fervent prayer of a righteous man availeth much.

JAMES 5:16

If we confess our sins, he is faithful and just to forgive us our sins, and to cleanse us from all unrighteousness.

1 JOHN 1:9

Whosoever therefore shall confess me before men, him will I confess also before my Father which is in heaven. But whosoever shall deny me before men, him will I also deny before my Father which is in heaven.

MATTHEW 10:32–33

Nevertheless, God's solid foundation stands firm, sealed with this inscription: "The Lord knows those who are his," and, "Everyone who confesses the name of the Lord must turn away from wickedness."

2 TIMOTHY 2:19 NIV

That if thou shalt confess with thy mouth the Lord Jesus, and shalt believe in thine heart that God hath raised him from the dead, thou shalt be saved. For with the heart man believeth unto righteousness; and with the mouth confession is made unto salvation.

ROMANS 10:9–10

Wherefore God also hath highly exalted him, and given him a name which is above every name: That at the name of Jesus every knee should bow, of things in heaven, and things in earth, and things under the earth; And that every tongue should confess that Jesus Christ is Lord, to the glory of God the Father.

PHILIPPIANS 2:9–11

For many deceivers are entered into the world, who confess not that Jesus Christ is come in the flesh. This is a deceiver and an antichrist.

2 JOHN 7

Whosoever shall confess that Jesus is the Son of God, God dwelleth in him, and he in God.

1 JOHN 4:15

Beloved, believe not every spirit, but try the spirits whether they are of God: because many false prophets are gone out into the world. Hereby know ye the Spirit of God: Every spirit that confesseth that Jesus Christ is come in the flesh is of God: And every spirit that confesseth not that Jesus Christ is come in the flesh is not of God: and this is that spirit of antichrist, whereof ye have heard that it should come; and even now already is it in the world.

1 JOHN 4:1–3

He that overcometh, the same shall be clothed in white raiment; and I will not blot out his name out of the book of life, but I will confess his name before my Father, and before his angels.

REVELATION 3:5

Q: Do you need to confess to someone whom you've wronged?

Confidence

Def.: 1. belief in the trustworthiness or reliability of a person or thing; firm trust; 2. being certain about the truth of something.

Faith involves an attitude of hope and confidence. But at its core, faith is trusting a person.

JOHN ORTBERG
FAITH AND DOUBT

For we are the circumcision, which worship God in the spirit, and rejoice in Christ Jesus, and have no confidence in the flesh.

PHILIPPIANS 3:3

It is better to trust in the LORD than to put confidence in man. It is better to trust in the LORD than to put confidence in princes.

PSALM 118:8–9

For you have been my hope, Sovereign LORD, my confidence since my youth.

PSALM 71:5 NIV

In the fear of the LORD is strong confidence: and his children shall have a place of refuge.

PROVERBS 14:26

For the LORD shall be thy confidence.

PROVERBS 3:26

I have confidence in you through the Lord.

GALATIANS 5:10

Trust ye not in a friend, put ye not confidence in a guide: keep the doors of thy mouth from her that lieth in thy bosom. For the son dishonoureth the father, the daughter riseth up against her mother, the daughter in law against her mother in law; a man's enemies are the men of his own house. Therefore I will look unto the LORD; I will wait for the God of my salvation: my God will hear me.

MICAH 7:5–7

For we are made partakers of Christ, if we hold the beginning of our confidence stedfast unto the end.

HEBREWS 3:14

Cast not away therefore your confidence, which hath great recompence of reward.

HEBREWS 10:35

Beloved, if our heart condemn us not, then have we confidence toward God.

1 JOHN 3:21

And this is the confidence that we have in him, that, if we ask any thing according to his will, he heareth us: And if we know that he hear us, whatsoever we ask, we know that we have the petitions that we desired of him.

1 JOHN 5:14–15

And now, little children, abide in him; that, when he shall appear, we may have confidence, and not be ashamed before him at his coming.

1 JOHN 2:28

Q: There are self-help courses to improve self-confidence, but how do you increase your confidence in Christ?

Conformity

If fifty million people say a foolish thing, it is still a foolish thing.

ANATOLE FRANCE

Whenever you find yourself on the side of the majority, it is time to pause and reflect.

MARK TWAIN

I beseech you therefore, brethren, by the mercies of God, that ye present your bodies a living sacrifice, holy, acceptable unto God, which is your reasonable service. And be not conformed to this world: but be ye transformed by the renewing of your mind, that ye may prove what is that good, and acceptable, and perfect, will of God.

ROMANS 12:1–2

As obedient children, do not conform to the evil desires you had when you lived in ignorance. But just as he who called you is holy, so be holy in all you do.

1 PETER 1:14–15 NIV

"And you will know that I am the LORD, for you have not followed my decrees or kept my laws but have conformed to the standards of the nations around you."

EZEKIEL 11:12 NIV

Whosoever therefore shall be ashamed of me and of my words in this adulterous and sinful generation; of him also shall the Son of man be ashamed, when he cometh in the glory of his Father with the holy angels.

MARK 8:38

Be ye not unequally yoked together with unbelievers: for what fellowship hath righteousness with unrighteousness? and what communion hath light with darkness? . . . Wherefore come out from among them, and be ye separate, saith the Lord, and touch not the unclean thing; and I will receive you. And will be a Father unto you, and ye shall be my sons and daughters, saith the Lord Almighty.

2 CORINTHIANS 6:14, 17–18

Q: How much are you willing to stand up and resist the pressure to conform to the world's ways?

Courage

The first step of courage isn't taken in the midst of a battle; it's taken when you're willing to walk onto the battlefield and face the unknown.

STEVEN CURTIS CHAPMAN
THE GREAT ADVENTURE

Be strong and of a good courage, fear not, nor be afraid of them: for the Lord thy God, he it is that doth go with thee; he will not fail thee, nor forsake thee.

DEUTERONOMY 31:6

Only be thou strong and very courageous, that thou mayest observe to do according to all the law, which Moses my servant commanded thee: turn not from it to the right hand or to the left, that thou mayest prosper withersoever thou goest.

JOSHUA 1:7

"Be strong and let us fight bravely for our people and the cities of our God. The LORD will do what is good in his sight."

2 SAMUEL 10:12 NIV

But Jesus immediately said to them: "Take courage! It is I. Don't be afraid."

MATTHEW 14:27 NIV

Be strong and courageous, be not afraid nor dismayed for the king of Assyria, nor for all the multitude that is with him: for there be more with us than with him: With him is an arm of flesh; but with us is the LORD our God to help us, and to fight our battles.

2 CHRONICLES 32:7–8

Now when they saw the boldness of Peter and John, and perceived that they were unlearned and ignorant men, they marvelled; and they took knowledge of them, that they had been with Jesus.

ACTS 4:13

But Christ is faithful as the Son over God's house. And we are his house, if indeed we hold firmly to our confidence and the hope in which we glory.

HEBREWS 3:6 NIV

Q: Do you have courage? Do you have faith—despite your fear—to trust that God will help you?

Criticism

Def.: Critic—from Greek *kritikos*, from *krites* (judge). Criticism—1. finding legitimate fault with something; 2. commonly, censuring in a belittling tone with the intention of discouraging.

If you never get criticized, chances are you aren't getting anything done.

CHARLES R. SWINDOLL
HAND ME ANOTHER BRICK

We want to avoid any criticism of the way we administer this liberal gift.

2 CORINTHIANS 8:20 NIV

O LORD my God, in thee do I put my trust: save me from all them that persecute me, and deliver me.

PSALM 7:1

"Blessed are you when people insult you, persecute you and falsely say all kinds of evil against you because of me."

MATTHEW 5:11 NIV

Remember the word that I said unto you, The servant is not greater than his lord. If they have persecuted me, they will also persecute you; if they have kept my saying, they will keep yours also.

JOHN 15:20

Ye have heard that it hath been said, Thou shalt love thy neighbour, and hate thine enemy. But I say unto you, Love your enemies, bless them that curse you, do good to them that hate you, and pray for them which despitefully use you, and persecute you.

Matthew 5:43–44

Q: Are you able to listen to and accept legitimate criticism? Are you able to ignore malicious criticism?

Cults

Def.: 1. Any religious sect with non-biblical teachings; 2. "Sociological cults" add destructive elements of excessive authority, control over members, and an us-versus-them mentality.

There are about 2,500 cults in America today. As many as 7,000,000 Americans have been in cults, or cult-like groups. Some 180,000 Americans are recruited into cults every year.

For many shall come in my name, saying, I am Christ; and shall deceive many.

MARK 13:6

As we said before, so say I now again, if any man preach any other gospel unto you than that ye have received, let him be accursed.

GALATIANS 1:9

For the time will come when people will not put up with sound doctrine. Instead, to suit their own desires, they will gather around them a great number of teachers to say what their itching ears want to hear. They will turn their ears away from the truth and turn aside to myths.

2 TIMOTHY 4:3–4 NIV

For I testify unto every man that heareth the words of the prophecy of this book, If any man shall add unto these things, God shall add unto him the plagues that are written in this book: And if any man shall take away from the words of the book of this prophecy, God shall take away his part out of the book of life, and out of the holy city, and from the things which are written in this book.

Revelation 22:18–19

For no one can lay any foundation other than the one already laid, which is Jesus Christ.

1 Corinthians 3:11 NIV

Who is a liar but he that denieth that Jesus is the Christ? He is antichrist, that denieth the Father and the Son.

1 John 2:22

Neither is there salvation in any other: for there is none other name under heaven given among men, whereby we must be saved.

Acts 4:12

See to it that no one takes you captive through hollow and deceptive philosophy, which depends on human tradition and the elemental spiritual forces of this world rather than on Christ.

Colossians 2:8 NIV

For this purpose the Son of God was manifested, that he might destroy the works of the devil.

1 John 3:8

Then if any man shall say unto you, Lo, here is Christ, or there; believe it not. For there shall arise false Christs, and false prophets, and shall shew great signs and wonders; insomuch that, if it were possible, they shall deceive the very elect. Behold, I have told you before. Wherefore if they shall say unto you, Behold, he is in the desert; go not forth: behold, he is in the secret chambers; believe it not.

MATTHEW 24:23–26

But evil men and seducers shall wax worse and worse, deceiving, and being deceived. But continue thou in the things which thou hast learned and hast been assured of, knowing of whom thou hast learned them.

2 TIMOTHY 3:13–14

For such are false apostles, deceitful workers, transforming themselves into the apostles of Christ. And no marvel; for Satan himself is transformed into an angel of light.

2 CORINTHIANS 11:13–14

Q: Which sects do you consider to be non-Christian cults? Which groups are literal mind-control cults?

Dancing

Dancing with the feet is one thing, but dancing with the heart is another.

UNKNOWN

To every thing there is a season, and a time to every purpose under the heaven. . . . A time to weep, and a time to laugh; a time to mourn, and a time to dance.

ECCLESIASTES 3:1, 4

And David danced before the LORD with all his might.

2 SAMUEL 6:14

Let them praise his name in the dance: let them sing praises unto him with the timbrel and harp.

PSALM 149:3

Then shall the virgin rejoice in the dance, both young men and old together: for I will turn their mourning into joy, and will comfort them, and make them rejoice from their sorrow.

JEREMIAH 31:13

And Miriam the prophetess, the sister of Aaron, took a timbrel in her hand; and all the women went out after her with timbrels and with dances.

EXODUS 15:20

Thou hast turned for me my mourning into dancing: thou hast put off my sackcloth, and girded me with gladness; to the end that my glory may sing praise to thee, and not be silent. O LORD my God, I will give thanks unto thee for ever.

PSALM 30:11–12

Q: Can dancing be a legitimate part of modern worship? How do you feel about dancing just for fun?

Dating

There are three possible parts to a date. . . entertainment, food, and affection. When the affection *is* the entertainment, we no longer call it dating.

UNKNOWN

A survey of American teens reveals that 95% of boys and 87% of girls felt that sex was either "moderately important" or "very important" in dating.

No verses in the Bible specifically refer to dating. In Bible times, young men and women did not date. Their marriages were arranged by their parents. Nevertheless, the scripture gives many principles and promises that pertain to the practice of dating.

Do not be misled: "Bad company corrupts good character."

1 CORINTHIANS 15:33 NIV

The integrity of the upright shall guide them: but the perverseness of transgressors shall destroy them.

PROVERBS 11:3

Blessed are the pure in heart: for they shall see God.

MATTHEW 5:8

Do not be yoked together with unbelievers. For what do righteousness and wickedness have in common? Or what fellowship can light have with darkness?

2 CORINTHIANS 6:14 NIV

Honour thy father and thy mother: that thy days may be long upon the land which the LORD thy God giveth thee.

EXODUS 20:12

Even a child is known by his doings, whether his work be pure, and whether it be right.

PROVERBS 20:11

I therefore. . .beseech you that ye walk worthy of the vocation wherewith ye are called.

EPHESIANS 4:1

But take heed lest by any means this liberty of yours become a stumbling block to them that are weak. And through thy knowledge shall the weak brother perish, for whom Christ died? But when ye sin so against the brethren, and wound their weak conscience, ye sin against Christ.

1 CORINTHIANS 8:9, 11–12

And walk in love, as Christ also hath loved us, and hath given himself for us an offering and a sacrifice to God for a sweetsmelling savour. But fornication, and all uncleanness, or covetousness, let it not be once named among you, as becometh saints.

EPHESIANS 5:2–3

How can a young person stay on the path of purity? By living according to your word. . . . I have hidden your word in my heart that I might not sin against you.

PSALM 119:9, 11 NIV

Q: Do you believe in dating? Why or why not?

Death

Maximus: I knew a man once who said, "Death smiles at us all. All a man can do is smile back."

FROM THE MOVIE *GLADIATOR*

Death to a good man is his release from the imprisonment of this world, and his departure to the enjoyments of another world.

MATTHEW HENRY

Precious in the sight of the LORD is the death of his saints.

PSALM 116:15

Yea, though I walk through the valley of the shadow of death, I will fear no evil: for thou art with me; thy rod and thy staff they comfort me.

PSALM 23:4

In a moment shall they die, and the people shall be troubled at midnight, and pass away: and the mighty shall be taken away without hand.

JOB 34:20

Wherefore, as by one man sin entered into the world, and death by sin; and so death passed upon all men, for that all have sinned.

ROMANS 5:12

89

For the wages of sin is death; but the gift of God is eternal life through Jesus Christ our Lord.

ROMANS 6:23

For since by man came death, by man came also the resurrection of the dead. For as in Adam all die, even so in Christ shall all be made alive.

1 CORINTHIANS 15:21–22

Jesus said unto her, I am the resurrection, and the life: he that believeth in me, though he were dead, yet shall he live: And whosoever liveth and believeth in me shall never die. Believest thou this?

JOHN 11:25–26

And as it is appointed unto men once to die, but after this the judgment: So Christ was once offered to bear the sins of many; and unto them that look for him shall he appear the second time without sin unto salvation.

HEBREWS 9:27–28

For if we believe that Jesus died and rose again, even so them also which sleep in Jesus will God bring with him.

1 THESSALONIANS 4:14

Beloved, now are we the sons of God, and it doth not yet appear what we shall be: but we know that, when he shall appear, we shall be like him; for we shall see him as he is.

1 JOHN 3:2

The last enemy that shall be destroyed is death.

1 CORINTHIANS 15:26

And death and hell were cast into the lake of fire. This is the second death.

REVELATION 20:14

And God shall wipe away all tears from their eyes; and there shall be no more death, neither sorrow, nor crying, neither shall there be any more pain: for the former things are passed away.

REVELATION 21:4.

O death, where is thy sting? O grave, where is thy victory? The sting of death is sin; and the strength of sin is the law. But thanks be to God, which giveth us the victory through our Lord Jesus Christ.

1 CORINTHIANS 15:55–57

Q: Are you afraid of dying? Why? Do the Bible's promises of Heaven comfort you?

Deceit

Def.: 1. the act of deceiving or misleading by concealing or misrepresenting the truth; to make a person believe what is false; 2. a dishonest trick or a ploy.

Yoda: Joined the Dark Side Dooku has. Lies, deceit, creating mistrust are his ways now.

FROM THE MOVIE *STAR WARS: ATTACK OF THE CLONES*

The words of their mouths are wicked and deceitful; they fail to act wisely or do good.

PSALM 36:3 NIV

The heart is deceitful above all things, and desperately wicked: who can know it? I the LORD search the heart, I try the reins, even to give every man according to his ways, and according to the fruit of his doings.

JEREMIAH 17:9–10

Deceitful men shall not live out half their days; but I will trust in thee.

PSALM 55:23

Faithful are the wounds of a friend; but the kisses of an enemy are deceitful.

PROVERBS 27:6

Favour is deceitful, and beauty is vain: but a woman that feareth the LORD, she shall be praised.

PROVERBS 31:30

He shall redeem their soul from deceit and violence: and precious shall their blood be in his sight.

PSALM 72:14

. . .neither was any deceit in his mouth.

ISAIAH 53:9

"Do not steal. Do not lie. Do not deceive one another."

LEVITICUS 19:11 NIV

Let no man deceive you with vain words: for because of these things cometh the wrath of God upon the children of disobedience.

EPHESIANS 5:6

For, "Whoever would love life and see good days must keep their tongue from evil and their lips from deceitful speech."

1 PETER 3:10 NIV

But exhort one another daily, while it is called To day; lest any of you be hardened through the deceitfulness of sin.

HEBREWS 3:13

Q: How do you feel when others are deceitful with you? Do you sometimes use deception?

Defeat

Let this be thy final lesson, monster—No man is e'er defeated till his last breath is drawn!

FROM THE COMIC BOOK *THE MIGHTY THOR*

The Bible teaches that there are no lost causes. No permanent pit-dwellers except those who refuse to leave.

BETH MOORE
GET OUT OF THAT PIT

For a just man falleth seven times, and riseth up again: but the wicked shall fall into mischief.

PROVERBS 24:16

He brought me up also out of an horrible pit, out of the miry clay, and set my feet upon a rock, and established my goings. And he hath put a new song in my mouth, even praise unto our God: many shall see it, and fear, and shall trust in the LORD.

PSALM 40:2-3

And he said unto me, My grace is sufficient for thee: for my strength is made perfect in weakness. Most gladly therefore will I rather glory in my infirmities, that the power of Christ may rest upon me.

2 CORINTHIANS 12:9

The very fact that you have lawsuits among you means you have been completely defeated already. Why not rather be wronged? Why not rather be cheated? Instead, you yourselves cheat and do wrong, and you do this to your brothers and sisters.

1 CORINTHIANS 6:7–8 NIV

Therefore we do not lose heart. Though outwardly we are wasting away, yet inwardly we are being renewed day by day.

2 CORINTHIANS 4:16 NIV

Q: Do you feel defeated and hardly wanting to try anymore? Can you trust God to help you?

Demons

There are two equal and opposite errors into which our race can fall about the devils. One is to disbelieve in their existence. The other is to believe, and to feel an excessive and unhealthy interest in them.

C.S. LEWIS
THE SCREWTAPE LETTERS

For we wrestle not against flesh and blood, but against principalities, against powers, against the rulers of the darkness of this world, against spiritual wickedness in high places. Wherefore take unto you the whole armour of God, that ye may be able to withstand in the evil day, and having done all, to stand.

EPHESIANS 6:12–13

Now the Spirit speaketh expressly, that in the latter times some shall depart from the faith, giving heed to seducing spirits, and doctrines of devils.

1 TIMOTHY 4:1

Beloved, believe not every spirit, but try the spirits whether they are of God. . . . Every spirit that confesseth not that Jesus Christ is come in the flesh is not of God.

1 JOHN 4:1, 3

Neither give place to the devil.

EPHESIANS 4:27

Be alert and of sober mind. Your enemy the devil prowls around like a roaring lion looking for someone to devour. Resist him, standing firm in the faith.

1 PETER 5:8–9 NIV

Submit yourselves therefore to God. Resist the devil, and he will flee from you.

JAMES 4:7

Jesus rebuked the demon, and it came out of the boy, and he was healed at that moment.

MATTHEW 17:18 NIV

They brought unto him many that were possessed with devils: and he cast out the spirits with his word, and healed all that were sick.

MATTHEW 8:16

So the devils besought him, saying, If thou cast us out, suffer us to go away into the herd of swine. And he said unto them, Go. And when they were come out, they went into the herd of swine: and, behold, the whole herd of swine ran violently down a steep place into the sea, and perished in the waters.

MATTHEW 8:31–32

Then he called his twelve disciples together, and gave them power and authority over all devils, and to cure diseases.

LUKE 9:1

The sacrifices of pagans are offered to demons, not to God, and I do not want you to be participants with demons.

1 CORINTHIANS 10:20 NIV

Thou believest that there is one God; thou doest well: the devils also believe, and tremble.

JAMES 2:19

Q: Do you have power and authority over the demons? If not, how do you get such power?

Depression

Def.: A state of extreme dejection or melancholy, with feelings of hopelessness and inadequacy; often accompanied by loss of appetite and insomnia.

Depression is nourished by a lifetime of ungrieved and unforgiven hurts.

PENELOPE SWEET

The Spirit of the Lord GOD is upon me; because the LORD hath anointed me to preach good tidings unto the meek; he hath sent me to bind up the brokenhearted, to proclaim liberty to the captives, and the opening of the prison to them that are bound. . .To appoint unto them that mourn in Zion, to give unto them beauty for ashes, the oil of joy for mourning, the garment of praise for the spirit of heaviness; that they might be called trees of righteousness, the planting of the LORD, that he might be glorified.

ISAIAH 61:1, 3

Surely he hath borne our griefs, and carried our sorrows: yet we did esteem him stricken, smitten of God, and afflicted. But he was wounded for our transgressions, he was bruised for our iniquities: the chastisement of our peace was upon him; and with his stripes we are healed.

ISAIAH 53:4–5

Ye are of God, little children, and have overcome them: because greater is he that is in you, than he that is in the world.

1 JOHN 4:4

Why art thou cast down, O my soul? and why art thou disquieted within me? hope thou in God: for I shall yet praise him, who is the health of my countenance, and my God.

PSALM 42:11

The human spirit can endure in sickness, but a crushed spirit who can bear?

PROVERBS 18:14 NIV

And Jesus came and spake unto them, saying, All power is given unto me in heaven and in earth.

MATTHEW 28:18

Thou wilt keep him in perfect peace, whose mind is stayed on thee: because he trusteth in thee.

ISAIAH 26:3

Whatsoever things are true, whatsoever things are honest, whatsoever things are just, whatsoever things are pure, whatsoever things are lovely, whatsoever things are of good report; if there be any virtue, and if there be any praise, think on these things.

PHILIPPIANS 4:8

For the joy of the LORD is your strength.

NEHEMIAH 8:10

He giveth power to the faint; and to them that have no might he increaseth strength.

ISAIAH 40:29

Peace I leave with you, my peace I give unto you: not as the world giveth, give I unto you. Let not your heart be troubled, neither let it be afraid.

JOHN 14:27

Q: Are you suffering from a prolonged sense of depression? Who can you reach out to for help?

Discouragement

Hope is a good thing, maybe the best of things, and no good thing ever dies.

FROM THE MOVIE *THE SHAWSHANK REDEMPTION*

Behold, the LORD thy God hath set the land before thee: go up and possess it, as the LORD God of thy fathers hath said unto thee; fear not, neither be discouraged.

DEUTERONOMY 1:21

I cried unto God with my voice, even unto God with my voice; and he gave ear unto me.

PSALM 77:1

But they that wait upon the LORD shall renew their strength; they shall mount up with wings as eagles; they shall run, and not be weary; and they shall walk, and not faint.

ISAIAH 40:31

Have not I commanded thee? Be strong and of a good courage; be not afraid, neither be thou dismayed: for the LORD thy God is with thee whithersoever thou goest.

JOSHUA 1:9

He healeth the broken in heart, and bindeth up their wounds.

PSALM 147:3

We are troubled on every side, yet not distressed; we are perplexed, but not in despair.... Knowing that he which raised up the Lord Jesus shall raise up us also by Jesus, and shall present us with you.

2 CORINTHIANS 4:8, 14

A merry heart doeth good like a medicine: but a broken spirit drieth the bones.

PROVERBS 17:22

A broken and a contrite heart, O God, thou wilt not despise.

PSALM 51:17

Q: Are you discouraged about something? Do you find that reading the Psalms helps you?

Divorce

Legal experts estimate that as many as one out of every three divorces begin as a result of indulgence in Internet porn or online affairs.

What children lose when their parents split is their family. It is a fallacy to think of divorce as something between a husband and wife.

MICHELE WEINER-DAVIS
DIVORCE BUSTING

She shall be his wife; he may not put her away all his days.

DEUTERONOMY 22:19

"The man who hates and divorces his wife," says the LORD, the God of Israel, "does violence to the one he should protect," says the LORD Almighty. So be on your guard, and do not be unfaithful.

MALACHI 2:16 NIV

And he saith unto them, Whosoever shall put away his wife, and marry another, committeth adultery against her. And if a woman shall put away her husband, and be married to another, she committeth adultery.

MARK 10:11–12

That is why a man leaves his father and mother and is united to his wife, and they become one flesh.

GENESIS 2:24 NIV

He saith unto them, Moses because of the hardness of your hearts suffered you to put away your wives: but from the beginning it was not so. And I say unto you, Whosoever shall put away his wife, except it be for fornication, and shall marry another, committeth adultery: and whoso marrieth her which is put away doth commit adultery.

MATTHEW 19:8–9

It hath been said, Whosoever shall put away his wife, let him give her a writing of divorcement: But I say unto you, That whosoever shall put away his wife, saving for the cause of fornication, causeth her to commit adultery: and whosoever shall marry her that is divorced committeth adultery.

MATTHEW 5:31–32

To the married I give this command (not I, but the Lord): A wife must not separate from her husband. But if she does, she must remain unmarried or else be reconciled to her husband. And a husband must not divorce his wife.

1 CORINTHIANS 7:10–11 NIV

Q: If your parents have divorced, have you taken the time to work through your grief and anger? If you have friends of divorced parents, how can you help them to grieve?

Doubt

The apostle Paul declared, "What I am saying is true and reasonable" (Acts 26:25 NIV). . . yet 70% of Christian teens have some reservations about the Bible's trustworthiness.

The whole point is *not* not ever doubting or questioning. It is that we walk it through and we find our God faithful.

BETH MOORE

The fool hath said in his heart, There is no God.

PSALM 14:1

I hate double-minded people, but I love your law.

PSALM 119:113 NIV

A double minded man is unstable in all his ways.

JAMES 1:8

Jesus saith unto him, Thomas, because thou hast seen me, thou hast believed: blessed are they that have not seen, and yet have believed.

JOHN 20:29

"Stop doubting and believe."

JOHN 20:27 NIV

And he saith unto them, Why are ye fearful, O ye of little faith? Then he arose, and rebuked the winds and the sea; and there was a great calm.

MATTHEW 8:26

But without faith it is impossible to please him: for he that cometh to God must believe that he is, and that he is a rewarder of them that diligently seek him.

HEBREWS 11:6

Your word, LORD, is eternal; it stands firm in the heavens. Your faithfulness continues through all generations.

PSALM 119:89–90 NIV

If any of you lack wisdom, let him ask of God, that giveth to all men liberally, and upbraideth not; and it shall be given him. But let him ask in faith, nothing wavering. For he that wavereth is like a wave of the sea driven with the wind and tossed. For let not that man think that he shall receive any thing of the Lord.

JAMES 1:5–7

Wherefore seeing we also are compassed about with so great a cloud of witnesses, let us lay aside every weight, and the sin which doth so easily beset us, and let us run with patience the race that is set before us, Looking unto Jesus the author and finisher of our faith.

HEBREWS 12:1–2

I will instruct thee and teach thee in the way which thou shalt go: I will guide thee with mine eye.

PSALM 32:8

Q: If you have specific doubts about the Bible, have you asked your pastor, youth pastor, or parent those questions?

Drug Abuse

A drug person can learn to cope with things like seeing their dead grandmother crawling up their leg with a knife in her teeth. But no one should be asked to handle this trip.

FROM THE MOVIE *FEAR AND LOATHING IN LAS VEGAS*

# of Americans 12 and older using illegal drugs in past month: 8.7
# of 19-25-year-old Americans using illegal drugs in past month: 19.6
# of drug-related deaths in America, 2011: 37,485

For God hath not given us the spirit of fear; but of power, and of love, and of a sound mind.

2 TIMOTHY 1:7

But every man is tempted, when he is drawn away of his own lust, and enticed. Then when lust hath conceived, it bringeth forth sin: and sin, when it is finished, bringeth forth death.

JAMES 1:14-15

For you have spent enough time in the past doing what pagans choose to do—living in debauchery, lust, drunkenness, orgies, carousing and detestable idolatry.

1 PETER 4:3 NIV

The Spirit of the Lord is upon me, because he hath anointed me to preach the gospel to the poor; he hath sent me to heal the brokenhearted, to preach deliverance to the captives, and recovering of sight to the blind, to set at liberty them that are bruised, To preach the acceptable year of the Lord.... And he began to say unto them, This day is this scripture fulfilled in your ears.... And they were all amazed, and spake among themselves, saying, What a word is this! for with authority and power he commandeth the unclean spirits, and they come out.

LUKE 4:18–19, 21, 36

And ye shall know the truth, and the truth shall make you free.... If the Son therefore shall make you free, ye shall be free indeed.

JOHN 8:32, 36

There hath no temptation taken you but such as is common to man: but God is faithful, who will not suffer you to be tempted above that ye are able; but will with the temptation also make a way to escape, that ye may be able to bear it.

1 CORINTHIANS 10:13

Q: Do you know anyone who's experimenting with illegal drugs? What can you do to help that person?

Enemies

Def.: persons or groups actively nursing hatred for or seeking to harm other persons or groups; ones opposed to or hostile to others.

You have enemies? Good. That means you've stood up for something, sometime in your life.

WINSTON CHURCHILL

Bless them that curse you, and pray for them which despitefully use you. And unto him that smiteth thee on the one cheek offer also the other; and him that taketh away thy cloak forbid not to take thy coat also.

LUKE 6:28–29

Do not repay anyone evil for evil. Be careful to do what is right in the eyes of everyone. If it is possible, as far as it depends on you, live at peace with everyone. Do not take revenge, my dear friends, but leave room for God's wrath, for it is written: "It is mine to avenge; I will repay," says the Lord.

ROMANS 12:17–19 NIV

Ye have heard that it hath been said, Thou shalt love thy neighbour, and hate thine enemy. But I say unto you, Love your enemies, bless them that curse you, do good to them that hate you, and pray for them which despitefully use you, and persecute you.

MATTHEW 5:43–44

When a man's ways please the LORD, he maketh even his enemies to be at peace with him.

PROVERBS 16:7

Then came Peter to him, and said, Lord, how oft shall my brother sin against me, and I forgive him? till seven times? Jesus saith unto him, I say not unto thee, Until seven times: but, Until seventy times seven.

MATTHEW 18:21–22

Judge not, and ye shall not be judged: condemn not, and ye shall not be condemned: forgive, and ye shall be forgiven.

LUKE 6:37

So that we may boldly say, The Lord is my helper, and I will not fear what man shall do unto me.

HEBREWS 13:6

The LORD shall cause thine enemies that rise up against thee to be smitten before thy face: they shall come out against thee one way, and flee before thee seven ways.

DEUTERONOMY 28:7

Through God we shall do valiantly: for he it is that shall tread down our enemies.

PSALM 60:12

Let those who love the LORD hate evil, for he guards the lives of his faithful ones and delivers them from the hand of the wicked.

PSALM 97:10 NIV

Q: While praying for God to stop your enemies from doing evil, can you still genuinely love them?

Envy

Def.: 1. A longing for the possessions, success, or qualities of someone else; 2. the feeling of dissatisfaction or resentment caused by such desire.

Hatred is active, and envy passive dislike; there is but one step from envy to hate.

JOHANN WOLFGANG VON GOETHE

A sound heart is the life of the flesh: but envy the rottenness of the bones.

PROVERBS 14:30

For where envying and strife is, there is confusion and every evil work.

JAMES 3:16

Let not thine heart envy sinners: but be thou in the fear of the LORD all the day long.

PROVERBS 23:17

Then he said to them, "Watch out! Be on your guard against all kinds of greed; life does not consist in an abundance of possessions."

LUKE 12:15 NIV

Envy thou not the oppressor, and choose none of his ways.

PROVERBS 3:31

Let your conversation be without covetousness; and be content with such things as ye have: for he hath said, I will never leave thee, nor forsake thee.

HEBREWS 13:5

Anger is cruel and fury overwhelming, but who can stand before jealousy?

PROVERBS 27:4 NIV

But among you there must not be even a hint of sexual immorality, or of any kind of impurity, or of greed, because these are improper for God's holy people.

EPHESIANS 5:3 NIV

I know what it is to be in need, and I know what it is to have plenty. I have learned the secret of being content in any and every situation, whether well fed or hungry, whether living in plenty or in want. I can do all this through him who gives me strength.

PHILIPPIANS 4:12–13 NIV

Q: Are you envious of someone else? Have you prayed for God to make you grateful?

Faith

% of American teens with very few doubts about their beliefs: 80

% of teens who feel "very" or "somewhat" close to God: 71

Faith is believing when common sense tells you not to. Don't you see?

FROM THE MOVIE MIRACLE ON 34TH STREET

Never try to have more faith—just get to know God better. And because God is faithful, the better you know him, the more you'll trust him.

JOHN ORTBERG
IF YOU WANT TO WALK ON WATER,
YOU'VE GOT TO GET OUT OF THE BOAT

Now faith is the substance of things hoped for, the evidence of things not seen.

HEBREWS 11:1

But without faith it is impossible to please him: for he that cometh to God must believe that he is, and that he is a rewarder of them that diligently seek him.

HEBREWS 11:6

And Jesus answering saith unto them, Have faith in God.

MARK 11:22

So then faith cometh by hearing, and hearing by the word of God.

ROMANS 10:17

For by grace are ye saved through faith; and that not of yourselves: it is the gift of God: Not of works, lest any man should boast.

EPHESIANS 2:8–9

. . .for whatsoever is not of faith is sin.

ROMANS 14:23

He replied, "Because you have so little faith. Truly I tell you, if you have faith as small as a mustard seed, you can say to this mountain, 'Move from here to there' and it will move. Nothing will be impossible for you."

MATTHEW 17:20 NIV

Wherein ye greatly rejoice, though now for a season, if need be, ye are in heaviness through manifold temptations: That the trial of your faith, being much more precious than of gold that perisheth, though it be tried with fire, might be found unto praise and honour and glory at the appearing of Jesus Christ: Whom having not seen, ye love; in whom, though now ye see him not, yet believing, ye rejoice with joy unspeakable and full of glory: Receiving the end of your faith, even the salvation of your souls.

1 PETER 1:6–9

Therefore being justified by faith, we have peace with God through our Lord Jesus Christ.

ROMANS 5:1

I am crucified with Christ: nevertheless I live; yet not I, but Christ liveth in me: and the life which I now live in the flesh I live by the faith of the Son of God, who loved me, and gave himself for me.

GALATIANS 2:20

Q: Do you worry about whether you have enough faith? What steps can you take to increase your faith?

Fame

You've got big dreams? You want fame? Well, fame costs. And right here is where you start paying in sweat.

FROM THE MOVIE *FAME*

Fame is a vapor, popularity an accident, and riches take wings. Only one thing endures and that is character.

HORACE GREELEY

So then neither is he that planteth any thing, neither he that watereth; but God that giveth the increase. Now he that planteth and he that watereth are one: and every man shall receive his own reward according to his own labour.

1 CORINTHIANS 3:7–8

Let no man deceive himself. If any man among you seemeth to be wise in this world, let him become a fool, that he may be wise. For the wisdom of this world is foolishness with God. For it is written, He taketh the wise in their own craftiness. And again, The Lord knoweth the thoughts of the wise, that they are vain. Therefore let no man glory in men.

1 CORINTHIANS 3:18–21

LORD, I have heard of your fame; I stand in awe of your deeds, LORD.

HABAKKUK 3:2 NIV

Thy name, O LORD, endureth for ever; and thy memorial, O LORD, throughout all generations.

PSALM 135:13

The memory of the just is blessed: but the name of the wicked shall rot.

PROVERBS 10:7

A good name is rather to be chosen than great riches, and loving favour rather than silver and gold.

PROVERBS 22:1

Q: Do you really want fame, notoriety, and a reputation—or to be recognized and appreciated by God?

Fear

According to a 2007 New America Media survey, American teenagers' biggest fears are:

- family breakdown (24%)
- local violence (22%)
- poverty (17%)
- global warming (14%)

Listen, nothing makes us more manic than when we're tempted to panic.

BETH MOORE
A BEAUTIFUL MIND

But now thus saith the LORD that created thee. . . Fear not: for I have redeemed thee, I have called thee by thy name; thou art mine. When thou passest through the waters, I will be with thee; and through the rivers, they shall not overflow thee: when thou walkest through the fire, thou shalt not be burned; neither shall the flame kindle upon thee.

ISAIAH 43:1–2

Fear thou not; for I am with thee: be not dismayed; for I am thy God: I will strengthen thee; yea, I will help thee; yea, I will uphold thee with the right hand of my righteousness.

ISAIAH 41:10

I sought the LORD, and he heard me, and delivered me from all my fears.

PSALM 34:4

The LORD is my light and my salvation; whom shall I fear? the LORD is the strength of my life; of whom shall I be afraid?

PSALM 27:1

Peace I leave with you, my peace I give unto you: not as the world giveth, give I unto you. Let not your heart be troubled, neither let it be afraid.

JOHN 14:27

For God hath not given us the spirit of fear; but of power, and of love, and of a sound mind.

2 TIMOTHY 1:7

Do not be anxious about anything, but in every situation, by prayer and petition, with thanksgiving, present your requests to God. And the peace of God, which transcends all understanding, will guard your hearts and your minds in Christ Jesus.

PHILIPPIANS 4:6–7 NIV

. . .for he hath said, I will never leave thee, nor forsake thee. So that we may boldly say, The Lord is my helper, and I will not fear what man shall do unto me.

HEBREWS 13:5–6

Q: What is your greatest fear? Are you able to trust God to take care of it?

Flattery

Def.: 1. exaggerated or insincere compliments, especially with the intention of gaining favor or favors; 2. to please or gratify someone's vanity.

Miss Moneypenny: Flattery will get you nowhere—but don't stop trying.

FROM THE MOVIE *DR. NO*

The LORD shall cut off all flattering lips, and the tongue that speaketh proud things.

PSALM 12:3

A lying tongue hateth those that are afflicted by it; and a flattering mouth worketh ruin.

PROVERBS 26:28

The transgression of the wicked saith within my heart, that there is no fear of God before his eyes. For he flattereth himself in his own eyes, until his iniquity be found to be hateful.

PSALM 36:1–2

Meddle not with him that flattereth with his lips.

PROVERBS 20:19

For such people are not serving our Lord Christ, but their own appetites. By smooth talk and flattery they deceive the minds of naive people.

ROMANS 16:18 NIV

He that rebuketh a man afterwards shall find more favour than he that flattereth with the tongue.

PROVERBS 28:23

A man that flattereth his neighbour spreadeth a net for his feet.

PROVERBS 29:5

These people are grumblers and faultfinders; they follow their own evil desires; they boast about themselves and flatter others for their own advantage.

JUDE 16 NIV

For there shall be no more any vain vision nor flattering divination within the house of Israel.

EZEKIEL 12:24

Q: How do you judge the difference between flattery and praise? Can you accept sincere praise?

Forgiveness

Nelson Mandela: Forgiveness liberates the soul. It removes fear. That is why it is such a powerful weapon.

FROM THE MOVIE *INVICTUS*

Every one says forgiveness is a lovely idea, until they have something to forgive.

C. S. LEWIS
MERE CHRISTIANITY

Forgiveness from God

Blessed is the one whose transgressions are forgiven, whose sins are covered. Blessed is the one whose sin the LORD does not count against them and in whose spirit is no deceit.

PSALM 32:1–2 NIV

Have mercy upon me, O God, according to thy lovingkindness: according unto the multitude of thy tender mercies blot out my transgressions. Wash me throughly from mine iniquity, and cleanse me from my sin.

PSALM 51:1–2

For I will be merciful to their unrighteousness, and their sins and their iniquities will I remember no more.

HEBREWS 8:12

I, even I, am he that blotteth out thy transgressions for mine own sake, and will not remember thy sins.

ISAIAH 43:25

Let the wicked forsake his way, and the unrighteous man his thoughts: and let him return unto the LORD, and he will have mercy upon him; and to our God, for he will abundantly pardon.

ISAIAH 55:7

He that covereth his sins shall not prosper: but whoso confesseth and forsaketh them shall have mercy.

PROVERBS 28:13

If we say that we have no sin, we deceive ourselves, and the truth is not in us. If we confess our sins, he is faithful and just to forgive us our sins, and to cleanse us from all unrighteousness.

1 JOHN 1:8–9

Praise the LORD, my soul, and forget not all his benefits— who forgives all your sins and heals all your diseases, who redeems your life from the pit and crowns you with love and compassion, who satisfies your desires with good things so that your youth is renewed like the eagle's.

PSALM 103:2–5 NIV

Forgiveness of each other

Blessed are the merciful: for they shall obtain mercy.

MATTHEW 5:7

And when ye stand praying, forgive, if ye have ought against any: that your Father also which is in heaven may forgive you your trespasses. But if ye do not forgive, neither will your Father which is in heaven forgive your trespasses.

MARK 11:25–26

But love ye your enemies, and do good, and lend, hoping for nothing again; and your reward shall be great, and ye shall be the children of the Highest: for he is kind unto the unthankful and to the evil.

LUKE 6:35

If thine enemy be hungry, give him bread to eat; and if he be thirsty, give him water to drink: For thou shalt heap coals of fire upon his head, and the LORD shall reward thee.

PROVERBS 25:21–22

And be ye kind one to another, tenderhearted, forgiving one another, even as God for Christ's sake hath forgiven you.

EPHESIANS 4:32

Take heed to yourselves: If thy brother trespass against thee, rebuke him; and if he repent, forgive him. And if he trespass against thee seven times in a day, and seven times in a day turn again to thee, saying, I repent; thou shalt forgive him.

LUKE 17:3–4

Then came Peter to him, and said, Lord, how oft shall my brother sin against me, and I forgive him? till seven times? Jesus saith unto him, I say not unto thee, Until seven times: but, Until seventy times seven.

MATTHEW 18:21–22

Q: Have you been forgiven? How did it feel? Is there someone you need to forgive?

Friends

Ah know ah been talkin' a lot about standin' on your own. And that's good. We all gotta do that. But. . .it's a lot easier to stand alone when you got friends to help you do it.

FROM THE COMIC BOOK X-MEN: LEGACY

There is a world of difference between being friendly to someone because they're useful to you and being someone's friend.

JOHN ORTBERG
EVERYBODY'S NORMAL TILL YOU GET TO KNOW THEM

Can two walk together, except they be agreed?

AMOS 3:3

A man that hath friends must shew himself friendly: and there is a friend that sticketh closer than a brother.

PROVERBS 18:24

Bear ye one another's burdens, and so fulfil the law of Christ.

GALATIANS 6:2

Faithful are the wounds of a friend; but the kisses of an enemy are deceitful.

PROVERBS 27:6

A friend loveth at all times.

PROVERBS 17:17

Whoever would foster love covers over an offense, but whoever repeats the matter separates close friends.

PROVERBS 17:9 NIV

If either of them falls down, one can help the other up. But pity anyone who falls and has no one to help them up.

ECCLESIASTES 4:10 NIV

Know ye not that the friendship of the world is enmity with God? whosoever therefore will be a friend of the world is the enemy of God.

JAMES 4:4

He that walketh with wise men shall be wise: but a companion of fools shall be destroyed.

PROVERBS 13:20

Do not forsake your friend or a friend of your family, and do not go to your relative's house when disaster strikes you—better a neighbor nearby than a relative far away.

PROVERBS 27:10 NIV

Finally, be ye all of one mind, having compassion one of another, love as brethren, be pitiful, be courteous: Not rendering evil for evil, or railing for railing: but contrariwise blessing; knowing that ye are thereunto called, that ye should inherit a blessing.

1 PETER 3:8–9

Rejoice with them that do rejoice, and weep with them that weep.

ROMANS 12:15

Q: Who do you count as your closest friends, and who are your truest friends? Are they the same people?

The Future

A 2012 Junior Achievement USA survey of 14–18-year-olds found only 18% believe they'll be financially independent by age 20. 44% of teens believed this in 2011.

Our future is not about what we have or don't have, or about what might happen or what might not happen. Our future is all about Who we know and how well we know Him.

CINDI MCMENAMIN
LETTING GOD MEET YOUR EMOTIONAL NEEDS

My son, forget not my law; but let thine heart keep my commandments: For length of days, and long life, and peace, shall they add to thee.

PROVERBS 3:1–2

And the world passeth away, and the lust thereof: but he that doeth the will of God abideth for ever.

1 JOHN 2:17

Commit thy works unto the LORD, and thy thoughts shall be established.

PROVERBS 16:3

A man's heart deviseth his way: but the LORD directeth his steps.

PROVERBS 16:9

Jesus said unto him, If thou canst believe, all things are possible to him that believeth.

MARK 9:23

Without counsel purposes are disappointed: but in the multitude of counsellors they are established.

PROVERBS 15:22

"For I know the plans I have for you," declares the LORD, "plans to prosper you and not to harm you, plans to give you hope and a future."

JEREMIAH 29:11 NIV

Do not let your heart envy sinners, but always be zealous for the fear of the LORD. There is surely a future hope for you, and your hope will not be cut off.

PROVERBS 23:17–18 NIV

In my Father's house are many mansions: if it were not so, I would have told you. I go to prepare a place for you. And if I go and prepare a place for you, I will come again, and receive you unto myself; that where I am, there ye may be also.

JOHN 14:2–3

Q: What can you do to prepare for the future? And what events do you have no control over?

Gambling

Def.: 1. Gamble—to play games of chance for money, especially for high stakes; to take great risks in the hope of substantial gain; 2. Any uncertain, risky undertaking.

Oh man. . . You better hold on to the coin you flipped. Because if this game keeps up like this, I'm going to have to borrow it.

FROM THE MOVIE *TWO FOR THE MONEY*

In the sweat of thy face shalt thou eat bread, till thou return unto the ground.

GENESIS 3:19

. . .for the children ought not to lay up for the parents, but the parents for the children.

2 CORINTHIANS 12:14

Whether therefore ye eat, or drink, or whatsoever ye do, do all to the glory of God.

1 CORINTHIANS 10:31

All things are lawful unto me, but all things are not expedient: all things are lawful for me, but I will not be brought under the power of any.

1 CORINTHIANS 6:12

If any would not work, neither should he eat.

2 THESSALONIANS 3:10

Set your affection on things above, not on things on the earth. . .fornication, uncleanness, inordinate affection, evil concupiscence, and covetousness, which is idolatry: For which things' sake the wrath of God cometh on the children of disobedience.

COLOSSIANS 3:2, 5–6

I beseech you therefore, brethren, by the mercies of God, that ye present your bodies a living sacrifice, holy, acceptable unto God, which is your reasonable service.

ROMANS 12:1

Thou shalt not steal. . . . Thou shalt not covet thy neighbour's house, thou shalt not covet thy neighbour's wife, nor his manservant, nor his maidservant, nor his ox, nor his ass, nor any thing that is thy neighbour's.

EXODUS 20:15, 17

Q: Do you believe you stand a chance of "getting rich quick"? Do you sometimes take shortcuts to success?

Gifts from God

God's gift to me is my potential. My gift back to God is what I do with my potential.

JOHN C. MAXWELL
DEVELOPING THE LEADER WITHIN YOU

Jesus answered and said unto her, If thou knewest the gift of God, and who it is that saith to thee, Give me to drink; thou wouldest have asked of him, and he would have given thee living water.

JOHN 4:10

The gift of God is eternal life through Jesus Christ our Lord.

ROMANS 6:23

For by grace are ye saved through faith; and that not of yourselves: it is the gift of God.

EPHESIANS 2:8

If ye then, being evil, know how to give good gifts unto your children: how much more shall your heavenly Father give the Holy Spirit to them that ask him?

LUKE 11:13

Wait for the promise of the Father, which, saith he, ye have heard of me.

ACTS 1:4

Then Peter said unto them, Repent, and be baptized every one of you in the name of Jesus Christ for the remission of sins, and ye shall receive the gift of the Holy Ghost. For the promise is unto you, and to your children, and to all that are afar off, even as many as the LORD our God shall call.

ACTS 2:38–39

But each of you has your own gift from God; one has this gift, another has that.

1 CORINTHIANS 7:7 NIV

We have different gifts, according to the grace given to each of us.

ROMANS 12:6 NIV

Now there are diversities of gifts, but the same Spirit. . . . And there are diversities of operations, but it is the same God which worketh all in all. But the manifestation of the Spirit is given to every man to profit withal.

1 CORINTHIANS 12:4, 6–7

And God hath set some in the church, first apostles, secondarily prophets, thirdly teachers, after that miracles, then gifts of healings, helps, governments, diversities of tongues. Are all apostles? are all prophets? are all teachers? are all workers of miracles? Have all the gifts of healing? do all speak with tongues? do all interpret? But covet earnestly the best gifts: and yet shew I unto you a more excellent way.

1 CORINTHIANS 12:28–31

Since you are eager for gifts of the Spirit, try to excel in those that build up the church.

1 CORINTHIANS 14:12 NIV

Neglect not the gift that is in thee, which was given thee by prophecy, with the laying on of the hands of the presbytery.

1 TIMOTHY 4:14

Stir up the gift of God, which is in thee.

2 TIMOTHY 1:6

Every good gift and every perfect gift is from above, and cometh down from the Father of lights, with whom is no variableness, neither shadow of turning.

JAMES 1:17

Each of you should use whatever gift you have received to serve others, as faithful stewards of God's grace in its various forms.

1 PETER 4:10 NIV

Q: God gives us gifts so that we can serve others. How can you use your gifts that way?

Giving

In a 2009 survey, 26% of Christian teens reported that they gave their own money to church; in 1997, 35% of Christian teens did so.

God has promised us that when we give, He will give back to us, then add some more.

JOEL OSTEEN
YOUR BEST LIFE NOW

Give, and it shall be given unto you; good measure, pressed down, and shaken together, and running over, shall men give into your bosom. For with the same measure that ye mete withal it shall be measured to you again.

LUKE 6:38

The righteous giveth and spareth not.

PROVERBS 21:26

Freely ye have received, freely give.

MATTHEW 10:8

One person gives freely, yet gains even more; another withholds unduly, but comes to poverty.

PROVERBS 11:24 NIV

Remember the words of the Lord Jesus, how he said, It is more blessed to give than to receive.

ACTS 20:35

Will a man rob God? Yet ye have robbed me. But ye say, Wherein have we robbed thee? In tithes and offerings. . . . Bring ye all the tithes into the storehouse, that there may be meat in mine house, and prove me now herewith, saith the LORD of hosts, if I will not open you the windows of heaven, and pour you out a blessing, that there shall not be room enough to receive it. And I will rebuke the devourer for your sakes.

MALACHI 3:8, 10–11

"And if anyone gives even a cup of cold water to one of these little ones who is my disciple, truly I tell you, that person will certainly not lose their reward."

MATTHEW 10:42 NIV

Every man according as he purposeth in his heart, so let him give; not grudgingly, or of necessity: for God loveth a cheerful giver.

2 CORINTHIANS 9:7

Honor the LORD with your wealth, with the firstfruits of all your crops; then your barns will be filled to overflowing, and your vats will brim over with new wine.

PROVERBS 3:9–10 NIV

A generous person will prosper; whoever refreshes others will be refreshed.

PROVERBS 11:25 NIV

Q: You may or may not believe in tithing—but do you know how Jesus said to give?

Goals

Anyway, a real plan is an actual goal that you believe in enough to create a set of circumstances. Which leads you to, and into, a plan. Comprende?

FROM THE MOVIE *HAVE DREAMS, WILL TRAVEL*

When you lay aside your personal goals, desires, and ambitions, that is when God will reveal the goals, desires, and ambitions that He has for you.

GREG LAURIE
THE UPSIDE DOWN CHURCH

Not as though I had already attained, either were already perfect. . .but this one thing I do, forgetting those things which are behind, and reaching forth unto those things which are before, I press toward the mark for the prize of the high calling of God in Christ Jesus.

PHILIPPIANS 3:12–14

So we make it our goal to please him, whether we are at home in the body or away from it.

2 CORINTHIANS 5:9 NIV

The goal of this command is love, which comes from a pure heart and a good conscience and a sincere faith.

1 TIMOTHY 1:5 NIV

Delight thyself also in the LORD: and he shall give thee the desires of thine heart. Commit thy way unto the LORD; trust also in him; and he shall bring it to pass.

PSALM 37:4–5

Do you not know that in a race all the runners run, but only one gets the prize? Run in such a way as to get the prize. Everyone who competes in the games goes into strict training. They do it to get a crown that will not last, but we do it to get a crown that will last forever.

1 CORINTHIANS 9:24–25 NIV

Wherefore seeing we also are compassed about with so great a cloud of witnesses, let us lay aside every weight, and the sin which doth so easily beset us, and let us run with patience the race that is set before us, looking unto Jesus the author and finisher of our faith; who for the joy that was set before him endured the cross, despising the shame, and is set down at the right hand of the throne of God.

HEBREWS 12:1–2

Let us not become weary in doing good, for at the proper time we will reap a harvest if we do not give up.

GALATIANS 6:9 NIV

Q: Have you found out yet whether you and God have the same goals for your life?

Gossip

Def.: 1. Casual conversation about social incidents or about people's personal matters; 2. Idle talk; malicious, unfounded rumors; 3. Tabloid columns or media spots discussing celebrities.

A gossip betrays a confidence; so avoid anyone who talks too much.

PROVERBS 20:19 NIV

A talebearer revealeth secrets: but he that is of a faithful spirit concealeth the matter.

PROVERBS 11:13

The words of a gossip are like choice morsels; they go down to the inmost parts.

PROVERBS 18:8 NIV

"Do not go about spreading slander among your people. . . . I am the LORD."

LEVITICUS 19:16 NIV

Where no wood is, there the fire goeth out: so where there is no talebearer, the strife ceaseth. As coals are to burning coals, and wood to fire; so is a contentious man to kindle strife.

PROVERBS 26:20–21

I said, I will take heed to my ways, that I sin not with my tongue.

PSALM 39:1

If any man among you seem to be religious, and bridleth not his tongue, but deceiveth his own heart, this man's religion is vain.

JAMES 1:26

These six things doth the LORD hate: yea, seven are an abomination unto him: A proud look, a lying tongue, and hands that shed innocent blood, An heart that deviseth wicked imaginations, feet that be swift in running to mischief, A false witness that speaketh lies, and he that soweth discord among brethren.

PROVERBS 6:16–19

Keep thy tongue from evil, and thy lips from speaking guile.

PSALM 34:13

Even so the tongue is a little member, and boasteth great things. Behold, how great a matter a little fire kindleth! Out of the same mouth proceedeth blessing and cursing. My brethren, these things ought not so to be.

JAMES 3:5, 10

Q: When you think of "gossip," what comes to mind? What motivates you to share news?

Grief

Christians sometimes think that we are not supposed to grieve, because our faith and theology provide us with confidence about heaven and eternal life. But. . .we grieve nevertheless. It is a legitimate response to loss.

ALBERT HSU
GRIEVING A SUICIDE

Blessed are they that mourn: for they shall be comforted.

MATTHEW 5:4

Jesus wept. Then said the Jews, Behold how he loved him!

JOHN 11:35–36

Let not your heart be troubled: ye believe in God, believe also in me.

JOHN 14:1

Blessed be the God and Father of our Lord Jesus Christ, which according to his abundant mercy hath begotten us again unto a lively hope by the resurrection of Jesus Christ from the dead, To an inheritance incorruptible, and undefiled, and that fadeth not away, reserved in heaven for you, Who are kept by the power of God through faith unto salvation ready to be revealed in the last time.

1 PETER 1:3–5

For we know that if our earthly house of this tabernacle were dissolved, we have a building of God, an house not made with hands, eternal in the heavens.

2 CORINTHIANS 5:1

Brothers and sisters, we do not want you to be uninformed about those who sleep in death, so that you do not grieve like the rest of mankind, who have no hope. For we believe that Jesus died and rose again, and so we believe that God will bring with Jesus those who have fallen asleep in him.

1 THESSALONIANS 4:13–14 NIV

Q: Have you grieved the loss of a friendship or a death? What measure of peace have you gained?

Guilt

Def.: 1. Being responsible for having committed an offense; 2. a sense of culpability, a feeling of having done wrong, of being deserving of blame.

Sin with the multitude, and your responsibility and guilt are as great and as truly personal, as if you alone had done the wrong.

TRYON EDWARDS

He that covereth his sins shall not prosper: but whoso confesseth and forsaketh them shall have mercy.

PROVERBS 28:13

When I kept silent, my bones wasted away through my groaning all day long. . . . Then I acknowledged my sin to you and did not cover up my iniquity. I said, "I will confess my transgressions to the LORD." And you forgave the guilt of my sin.

PSALM 32:3, 5 NIV

Although you wash yourself with soap and use an abundance of cleansing powder, the stain of your guilt is still before me," declares the Sovereign LORD.

JEREMIAH 2:22 NIV

For whosoever shall keep the whole law, and yet offend in one point, he is guilty of all.

JAMES 2:10

Come now, and let us reason together, saith the LORD: though your sins be as scarlet, they shall be as white as snow; though they be red like crimson, they shall be as wool.

ISAIAH 1:18

As far as the east is from the west, so far hath he removed our transgressions from us.

PSALM 103:12

My guilt has overwhelmed me like a burden too heavy to bear.

PSALM 38:4 NIV

For if ye turn again unto the LORD, your brethren and your children shall find compassion before them that lead them captive, so that they shall come again into this land: for the LORD your God is gracious and merciful, and will not turn away his face from you, if ye return unto him.

2 CHRONICLES 30:9

If we say that we have fellowship with him, and walk in darkness, we lie, and do not the truth: But if we walk in the light, as he is in the light, we have fellowship one with another, and the blood of Jesus Christ his Son cleanseth us from all sin.

1 JOHN 1:6–7

Thine iniquity is taken away, and thy sin purged.

ISAIAH 6:7

There is therefore now no condemnation to them which are in Christ Jesus, who walk not after the flesh, but after the Spirit.

ROMANS 8:1

Therefore, brothers and sisters, since we have confidence to enter the Most Holy Place by the blood of Jesus. . . let us draw near to God with a sincere heart and with the full assurance that faith brings, having our hearts sprinkled to cleanse us from a guilty conscience and having our bodies washed with pure water.

HEBREWS 10:19, 22 NIV

Q: Some people think guilt is only a negative emotion—but what benefit can it bring about?

Healing

A 2012 Fox News Poll shows that 77% of voters believe prayer can help heal someone from illness or injury; 29% don't believe; 3% are uncertain.

Those who claim to believe in healing, but say one word in favor of it and ten words against it, cannot produce faith for healing.

F. F. BOSWORTH
CHRIST THE HEALER

Is any among you afflicted? let him pray. . . . Is any sick among you? let him call for the elders of the church; and let them pray over him, anointing him with oil in the name of the Lord: And the prayer of faith shall save the sick, and the Lord shall raise him up; and if he have committed sins, they shall be forgiven him. Confess your faults one to another, and pray one for another, that ye may be healed. The effectual fervent prayer of a righteous man availeth much.

JAMES 5:13–16

Then he called his twelve disciples together, and gave them power and authority over all devils, and to cure diseases. And he sent them to preach the kingdom of God, and to heal the sick.

LUKE 9:1–2

If thou wilt diligently hearken to the voice of the LORD thy God, and wilt do that which is right in his sight, and wilt give ear to his commandments, and keep all his statutes, I will put none of these diseases upon thee, which I have brought upon the Egyptians: for I am the LORD that healeth thee.

EXODUS 15:26

Bless the LORD, O my soul: and all that is within me, bless his holy name. . . . Who forgiveth all thine iniquities; who healeth all thy diseases.

PSALM 103:1, 3

He healeth the broken in heart, and bindeth up their wounds.

PSALM 147:3

"But I will restore you to health and heal your wounds," declares the LORD.

JEREMIAH 30:17 NIV

He gives strength to the weary and increases the power of the weak. . .those who hope in the LORD will renew their strength.

ISAIAH 40:29, 31 NIV

He healeth the broken in heart, and bindeth up their wounds.

PSALM 147:3

And Jesus went about all Galilee. . .healing all manner of sickness and all manner of disease among the people.

MATTHEW 4:23

And Jesus went about all the cities and villages, teaching in their synagogues, and preaching the gospel of the kingdom, and healing every sickness and every disease among the people.

MATTHEW 9:35

But he was wounded for our transgressions, he was bruised for our iniquities: the chastisement of our peace was upon him; and with his stripes we are healed.

ISAIAH 53:5

Who his own self bare our sins in his own body on the tree, that we, being dead to sins, should live unto righteousness: by whose stripes ye were healed.

1 PETER 2:24

When Jesus saw him. . .and knew that he had been now a long time in that case, he saith unto him, Wilt thou be made whole?

JOHN 5:6

The apostles performed many signs and wonders among the people. . . . Crowds gathered also from the towns around Jerusalem, bringing their sick and those tormented by impure spirits, and all of them were healed.

ACTS 5:12, 16 NIV

Q: Has God ever physically healed you or a loved one? Do you need His touch now?

Heaven

Of 12–19 year-old American teens surveyed in 2007, 69% believe that heaven exists.

Heaven is not a state of mind. Heaven is reality itself.

C.S. LEWIS
THE GREAT DIVORCE

You have come to Mount Zion, to the city of the living God, the heavenly Jerusalem. You have come to thousands upon thousands of angels in joyful assembly.

HEBREWS 12:22 NIV

For Christ did not enter a sanctuary made with human hands that was only a copy of the true one; he entered heaven itself, now to appear for us in God's presence.

HEBREWS 9:24 NIV

In my Father's house are many mansions: if it were not so, I would have told you. I go to prepare a place for you. And if I go and prepare a place for you, I will come again, and receive you unto myself; that where I am, there ye may be also.

JOHN 14:2–3

But now they desire a better country, that is, an heavenly: wherefore God is not ashamed to be called their God: for he hath prepared for them a city.

HEBREWS 11:16

Beloved, now are we the sons of God, and it doth not yet appear what we shall be: but we know that, when he shall appear, we shall be like him; for we shall see him as he is.

1 JOHN 3:2

But as it is written, Eye hath not seen, nor ear heard, neither have entered into the heart of man, the things which God hath prepared for them that love him.

1 CORINTHIANS 2:9

Behold, I shew you a mystery; We shall not all sleep, but we shall all be changed, In a moment, in the twinkling of an eye, at the last trump: for the trumpet shall sound, and the dead shall be raised incorruptible, and we shall be changed.

1 CORINTHIANS 15:51–52

And I say unto you, That many shall come from the east and west, and shall sit down with Abraham, and Isaac, and Jacob, in the kingdom of heaven.

MATTHEW 8:11

After this I beheld, and, lo, a great multitude, which no man could number, of all nations, and kindreds, and people, and tongues, stood before the throne, and before the Lamb, clothed with white robes, and palms in their hands.

REVELATION 7:9

And they sing the song of Moses the servant of God, and the song of the Lamb, saying, Great and marvellous are thy works, Lord God Almighty; just and true are thy ways, thou King of saints.

REVELATION 15:3

And God shall wipe away all tears from their eyes; and there shall be no more death, neither sorrow, nor crying, neither shall there be any more pain: for the former things are passed away.

REVELATION 21:4

And I saw no temple therein: for the Lord God Almighty and the Lamb are the temple of it. And the city had no need of the sun, neither of the moon, to shine in it: for the glory of God did lighten it, and the Lamb is the light thereof. And the nations of them which are saved shall walk in the light of it: and the kings of the earth do bring their glory and honour into it

REVELATION 21:22–24

Q: Are you certain that you're going to heaven? If not, how can you become certain?

Hell

In a 2009 survey of Americans, 74% believed in heaven; only 59% believed in hell.

The main reason we believe in hell is because Jesus Christ declares that it is so.

D. JAMES KENNEDY
WHY I BELIEVE

The wicked shall be turned into hell, and all the nations that forget God.

PSALM 9:17

Stolen waters are sweet, and bread eaten in secret is pleasant. But he knoweth not that the dead are there; and that her guests are in the depths of hell.

PROVERBS 9:17–18

God spared not the angels that sinned, but cast them down to hell, and delivered them into chains of darkness, to be reserved unto judgment.

2 PETER 2:4

Enter ye in at the strait gate: for wide is the gate, and broad is the way, that leadeth to destruction, and many there be which go in thereat.

MATTHEW 7:13

Ye have heard that it was said of them of old time, Thou shalt not kill; and whosoever shall kill shall be in danger of the judgment: But I say unto you, That whosoever is angry with his brother without a cause shall be in danger of the judgment: and whosoever shall say to his brother, Raca, shall be in danger of the council: but whosoever shall say, Thou fool, shall be in danger of hell fire.

MATTHEW 5:21–22

How shall we escape, if we neglect so great salvation?

HEBREWS 2:3

And if thy hand offend thee, cut it off: it is better for thee to enter into life maimed, than having two hands to go into hell, into the fire that never shall be quenched: Where their worm dieth not, and the fire is not quenched.

MARK 9:43–44

And beside all this, between us and you there is a great gulf fixed: so that they which would pass from hence to you cannot; neither can they pass to us, that would come from thence.

LUKE 16:26

And I say unto you my friends, Be not afraid of them that kill the body, and after that have no more that they can do. But I will forewarn you whom ye shall fear: Fear him, which after he hath killed hath power to cast into hell; yea, I say unto you, Fear him.

LUKE 12:4–5

And the beast was taken, and with him the false prophet that wrought miracles before him, with which he deceived them that had received the mark of the beast, and them that worshipped his image. These both were cast alive into a lake of fire burning with brimstone.

REVELATION 19:20

He will punish those who do not know God and do not obey the gospel of our Lord Jesus. They will be punished with everlasting destruction and shut out from the presence of the Lord and from the majesty of his power.

2 THESSALONIANS 1:8–9 NIV

And death and hell were cast into the lake of fire. This is the second death. And whosoever was not found written in the book of life was cast into the lake of fire.

REVELATION 20:14–15

He that overcometh shall inherit all things; and I will be his God, and he shall be my son. But the fearful, and unbelieving, and the abominable, and murderers, and whoremongers, and sorcerers, and idolaters, and all liars, shall have their part in the lake which burneth with fire and brimstone: which is the second death.

REVELATION 21:7–8

Q: What do you personally believe about hell? What do you think it's like?

Home

All of life is a coming home. Salesmen, secretaries, coal miners, beekeepers, sword swallowers, all of us. All the restless hearts of the world, all trying to find a way home.

FROM THE MOVIE *PATCH ADAMS*

A truly Christian home is a place where sinners live; but it is also a place where the members of that home admit that fact and understand the problem, know what to do about it, and as a result grow by grace.

JAY ADAMS
CHRISTIAN LIVING IN THE HOME

These commandments that I give you today are to be on your hearts. Impress them on your children. Talk about them when you sit at home and when you walk along the road, when you lie down and when you get up.

DEUTERONOMY 6:6–7 NIV

For I know him, that he will command his children and his household after him, and they shall keep the way of the LORD, to do justice and judgment; that the LORD may bring upon Abraham that which he hath spoken of him.

GENESIS 18:19

Train up a child in the way he should go: and when he is old, he will not depart from it.

PROVERBS 22:6

And if it seem evil unto you to serve the LORD, choose you this day whom ye will serve; whether the gods which your fathers served that were on the other side of the flood, or the gods of the Amorites, in whose land ye dwell: but as for me and my house, we will serve the LORD.

JOSHUA 24:15

I will behave myself wisely in a perfect way. O when wilt thou come unto me? I will walk within my house with a perfect heart.

PSALM 101:2

But if a widow has children or grandchildren, these should learn first of all to put their religion into practice by caring for their own family and so repaying their parents and grandparents, for this is pleasing to God.

1 TIMOTHY 5:4 NIV

Be careful to obey all these regulations I am giving you, so that it may always go well with you and your children after you, because you will be doing what is good and right in the eyes of the LORD your God.

DEUTERONOMY 12:28 NIV

Better is a dry morsel, and quietness therewith, than an house full of sacrifices with strife.

PROVERBS 17:1

Children, obey your parents in the Lord: for this is right. Honour thy father and mother; which is the first commandment with promise; That it may be well with thee, and thou mayest live long on the earth. And, ye fathers, provoke not your children to wrath: but bring them up in the nurture and admonition of the Lord.

EPHESIANS 6:1–4

Q: What are the most important things about home for you? What things do you take for granted?

Homosexuality

Anyone who takes the Bible seriously knows that it is. . .intolerant of sexual sins among heterosexuals and homosexuals; it loudly discriminates against those who do a variety of evils and those who believe false doctrine.

ERWIN W. LUTZER
THE TRUTH ABOUT SAME-SEX MARRIAGE

Do you not know that wrongdoers will not inherit the kingdom of God? Do not be deceived: Neither the sexually immoral nor idolaters nor adulterers nor men who have sex with men nor thieves nor the greedy nor drunkards nor slanderers nor swindlers will inherit the kingdom of God.

1 CORINTHIANS 6:9–10 NIV

Thou shalt not lie with mankind, as with womankind: it is abomination.

LEVITICUS 18:22

"If a man has sexual relations with a man as one does with a woman, both of them have done what is detestable. They are to be put to death; their blood will be on their own heads."

LEVITICUS 20:13 NIV

Wherefore God also gave them up to uncleanness through the lusts of their own hearts, to dishonour their own bodies between themselves: Who changed the truth of God into a lie, and worshipped and served the creature more than the Creator, who is blessed for ever. Amen. For this cause God gave them up unto vile affections: for even their women did change the natural use into that which is against nature: And likewise also the men, leaving the natural use of the woman, burned in their lust one toward another; men with men working that which is unseemly, and receiving in themselves that recompence of their error which was meet. . . . Who knowing the judgment of God, that they which commit such things are worthy of death, not only do the same, but have pleasure in them that do them.

ROMANS 1:24–27, 32

And that is what some of you were. But you were washed, you were sanctified, you were justified in the name of the Lord Jesus Christ and by the Spirit of our God.

1 CORINTHIANS 6:11 NIV

Q: As Christians we say we "hate the sin, but love the sinner." Do you truly hate sexual sins? Do you truly love those who commit sex sin?

Honesty

8% of American teens say they have obtained or shared music illegally; 77% of Christian teens have done the same.

A lie keeps growing and growing until it's as plain as the nose on your face.

FROM THE MOVIE PINOCCHIO

Now the parable is this: The seed is the word of God. But that on the good ground are they, which in an honest and good heart, having heard the word, keep it, and bring forth fruit with patience.

LUKE 8:11, 15

Thou knowest the commandments, Do not commit adultery, Do not kill, Do not steal, Do not bear false witness, Defraud not, Honour thy father and mother.

MARK 10:19

"Do not use dishonest standards when measuring length, weight or quantity. Use honest scales and honest weights, an honest ephah and an honest hin. I am the LORD your God, who brought you out of Egypt."

LEVITICUS 19:35–36 NIV

Avoiding this, that no man should blame us in this abundance which is administered by us: Providing for honest things, not only in the sight of the Lord, but also in the sight of men.

2 CORINTHIANS 8:20–21

Thou shalt not have in thine house divers measures, a great and a small. But thou shalt have a perfect and just weight, a perfect and just measure shalt thou have: that thy days may be lengthened in the land which the LORD thy God giveth thee. For all that do such things, and all that do unrighteously, are an abomination unto the LORD thy God.

DEUTERONOMY 25:14–16

Who shall ascend into the hill of the LORD? or who shall stand in his holy place? He that hath clean hands, and a pure heart; who hath not lifted up his soul unto vanity, nor sworn deceitfully.

PSALM 24:3–4

An honest witness tells the truth, but a false witness tells lies.

PROVERBS 12:17 NIV

And herein do I exercise myself, to have always a conscience void to offence toward God, and toward men.

ACTS 24:16

Pray for us: for we trust we have a good conscience, in all things willing to live honestly.

HEBREWS 13:18

Better is a little with righteousness than great revenues without right.

PROVERBS 16:8

Q: Are you honest in word and in deed all of the time, most of the time, or some of the time?

Humility

Def.: the condition or quality of being humble; lowliness of mind; a modest estimation of one's worth; a lack of pride and arrogance.

Humble has two meanings: it means "not proud" and it also means "near the ground." That's Wilbur all over.

FROM THE MOVIE *CHARLOTTE'S WEB*

Let this mind be in you, which was also in Christ Jesus: Who, being in the form of God, thought it not robbery to be equal with God: But made himself of no reputation, and took upon him the form of a servant, and was made in the likeness of men: And being found in fashion as a man, he humbled himself, and became obedient unto death, even the death of the cross.

PHILIPPIANS 2:5–8

If my people, which are called by my name, shall humble themselves, and pray, and seek my face, and turn from their wicked ways; then will I hear from heaven, and will forgive their sin, and will heal their land.

2 CHRONICLES 7:14

He mocks proud mockers but shows favor to the humble and oppressed.

PROVERBS 3:34 NIV

The fear of the LORD is the instruction of wisdom; and before honour is humility.

PROVERBS 15:33

By humility and the fear of the LORD are riches, and honour, and life.

PROVERBS 22:4

Now Moses was a very humble man, more humble than anyone else on the face of the earth.

NUMBERS 12:3 NIV

I tell you, this man went down to his house justified rather than the other: for every one that exalteth himself shall be abased; and he that humbleth himself shall be exalted.

LUKE 18:14

Whosoever therefore shall humble himself as this little child, the same is greatest in the kingdom of heaven.

MATTHEW 18:4

But he giveth more grace. Wherefore he saith, God resisteth the proud, but giveth grace unto the humble.

JAMES 4:6

Humble yourselves, therefore, under God's mighty hand, that he may lift you up in due time.

1 PETER 5:6 NIV

Q: Do you have a modest estimation of your worth—or are you still working on this virtue?

Hypocrisy

Def.: from the Greek words for "play a part; pretend." To pretend that one has virtues, emotions, or faith that one does not actually possess.

There is something insincere about a man or woman who repeatedly tells God how much he or she loves Him while refusing to obey Him.

ANDY STANLEY
LOUDER THAN WORDS

Their inward part is very wickedness; their throat is an open sepulchre; they flatter with their tongue.

PSALM 5:9

Wherefore the LORD said, Forasmuch as this people draw near me with their mouth, and with their lips do honour me, but have removed their heart far from me.

ISAIAH 29:13

"Woe to you, teachers of the law and Pharisees, you hypocrites! You travel over land and sea to win a single convert, and when you have suceeded, you make them twice as much a child of hell as you are."

MATTHEW 23:15 NIV

They profess that they know God; but in works they deny him, being abominable, and disobedient, and unto every good work reprobate.

Titus 1:16

"Why do you look at the speck of sawdust in your brother's eye and pay no attention to the plank in your own eye? How can you say to your brother, 'Brother, let me take the speck out of your eye,' when you yourself fail to see the plank in your own eye? You hypocrite, first take the plank out of your eye, and then you will see clearly to remove the speck from your brother's eye."

Luke 6:41–42 NIV

Woe unto you, scribes and Pharisees, hypocrites! for ye devour widows' houses, and for a pretence make long prayer: therefore ye shall receive the greater damnation.

Matthew 23:14

Woe unto you, scribes and Pharisees, hypocrites! for ye pay tithe of mint and anise and cummin, and have omitted the weightier matters of the law, judgment, mercy, and faith: these ought ye to have done, and not to leave the other undone. Ye blind guides, which strain at a gnat, and swallow a camel.

Matthew 23:23–24

Lord, who shall abide in thy tabernacle? who shall dwell in thy holy hill? He that walketh uprightly, and worketh righteousness, and speaketh the truth in his heart.

Psalm 15:1–2

"Woe to you, teachers of the law and Pharisees, you hypocrites! You clean the outside of the cup and dish, but inside they are full of greed and self-indulgence. Blind Pharisee! First clean the inside of the cup and dish, and then the outside also will be clean."

MATTHEW 23:25–26 NIV

Woe unto you, scribes and Pharisees, hypocrites! for ye are like unto whited sepulchres, which indeed appear beautiful outward, but are within full of dead men's bones, and of all uncleanness. Even so ye also outwardly appear righteous unto men, but within ye are full of hypocrisy and iniquity.

MATTHEW 23:27–28

Q: Are you a hypocrite in any area of your life? Are you praying for God to change you?

Incest

Def.: sexual activity between close relatives

"No one is to approach any close relative to have sexual relations. I am the Lord. Do not dishonor your father by having sexual relations with your mother. She is your mother; do not have relations with her."

LEVITICUS 18:6–7 NIV

"Do not have sexual relations with your sister, either your father's daughter or your mother's daughter, whether she was born in the same home or elsewhere. Do not have sexual relations with your son's daughter or your daughter's daughter; that would dishonor you. Do not have sexual relations with the daughter of your father's wife, born to your father; she is your sister. Do not have sexual relations with your father's sister; she is your father's close relative. Do not have sexual relations with your mother's sister, because she is your mother's close relative. Do not dishonor your father's brother by approaching his wife to have sexual relations; she is your aunt. Do not have sexual relations with your daughter-in-law. She is your son's wife; do not have relations with her. Do not have sexual relations with your brother's wife; that would dishonor your brother. Do not have sexual relations with both a woman and her daughter. Do not have sexual relations with either her son's daughter or her daughter's daughter; they are her close relatives. That is wickedness. Do not take your wife's sister as a rival wife and have sexual relations with her while your wife is living."

LEVITICUS 18:9–18 NIV

"Everyone who does any of these detestable things—such persons must be cut off from their people."

Leviticus 18:29 NIV

For the victims of incest

When my father and my mother forsake me, then the LORD will take me up.

Psalm 27:10

Fear thou not; for I am with thee: be not dismayed; for I am thy God: I will strengthen thee; yea, I will help thee; yea, I will uphold thee with the right hand of my righteousness. Behold, all they that were incensed against thee shall be ashamed and confounded: they shall be as nothing; and they that strive with thee shall perish. For I the LORD thy God will hold thy right hand, saying unto thee, Fear not; I will help thee.

Isaiah 41:10–11, 13

Do not be anxious about anything, but in every situation, by prayer and petition, with thanksgiving, present your requests to God. And the peace of God, which transcends all understanding, will guard your hearts and your minds in Christ Jesus.

Philippians 4:6–7 NIV

Q: How aware are you of the heavy toll this sin takes, psychologically and spiritually, on those victimized by it?

Laziness

All I do is eat and sleep. Eat and sleep. Eat and sleep. There must be more to a cat's life than that. But I hope not.

CARTOON CHARACTER GARFIELD

I was taught that laziness was one of the worst evils, and that there was dignity and honor in labor.

BILLY GRAHAM
JUST AS I AM

Laziness brings on deep sleep, and the shiftless go hungry.

PROVERBS 19:15 NIV

He becometh poor that dealeth with a slack hand: but the hand of the diligent maketh rich. He that gathereth in summer is a wise son: but he that sleepeth in harvest is a son that causeth shame.

PROVERBS 10:4–5

And withal they learn to be idle, wandering about from house to house; and not only idle, but tattlers also and busybodies, speaking things which they ought not.

1 TIMOTHY 5:13

Through laziness, the rafters sag; because of idle hands, the house leaks.

ECCLESIASTES 10:18 NIV

Go to the ant, thou sluggard; consider her ways, and be wise. . . . How long wilt thou sleep, O sluggard? when wilt thou arise out of thy sleep?

PROVERBS 6:6, 9

Poverty and shame shall be to him that refuseth instruction: but he that regardeth reproof shall be honoured.

PROVERBS 13:18

A little sleep, a little slumber, a little folding of the hands to rest—and poverty will come on you like a thief and scarcity like an armed man.

PROVERBS 6:10–11 NIV

He also that is slothful in his work is brother to him that is a great waster.

PROVERBS 18:9

We do not want you to become lazy, but to imitate those who through faith and patience inherit what has been promised.

HEBREWS 6:12 NIV

Q: On a scale of 1 to 10, how lazy do you consider yourself? How hard working?

Loneliness

I'm not lonely, I'm alone.

FROM THE MOVIE *ONE DAY*

Pray that your loneliness may spur you into finding something to live for, great enough to die for.

DAG HAMMARSKJÖLD

A father to the fatherless, a defender of widows, is God in his holy dwelling. God sets the lonely in families.

PSALM 68:5–6 NIV

God is our refuge and strength, a very present help in trouble. Therefore will not we fear, though the earth be removed, and though the mountains be carried into the midst of the sea; though the waters thereof roar and be troubled, though the mountains shake with the swelling thereof.

PSALM 46:1–3

And, behold, I am with thee, and will keep thee in all places whither thou goest, and will bring thee again into this land; for I will not leave thee, until I have done that which I have spoken to thee of.

GENESIS 28:15

And ye are complete in him, which is the head of all
principality and power.

COLOSSIANS 2:10

I will not leave you comfortless: I will come to you.

JOHN 14:18

I will never leave thee, nor forsake thee. So that we may
boldly say, The Lord is my helper, and I will not fear what
man shall do unto me.

HEBREWS 13:5–6

Lo, I am with you always, even unto the end of the world.
Amen.

MATTHEW 28:20

Q: Do you know any lonely people? Have you
considered spending time with them?

Love

Love is made by God. Ignore it and you suffer as you cannot imagine.

FROM THE MOVIE *TRISTAN AND ISOLDE*

It is impossible to love God without loving our neighbor.

MOTHER TERESA
LOVING JESUS

And we have known and believed the love that God hath to us. God is love; and he that dwelleth in love dwelleth in God, and God in him.

1 JOHN 4:16

For God so loved the world, that he gave his only begotten Son, that whosoever believeth in him should not perish, but have everlasting life.

JOHN 3:16

But God, who is rich in mercy, for his great love wherewith he loved us, Even when we were dead in sins, hath quickened us together with Christ, (by grace ye are saved;) And hath raised us up together, and made us sit together in heavenly places in Christ Jesus.

EPHESIANS 2:4–6

Herein is love, not that we loved God, but that he loved us, and sent his Son to be the propitiation for our sins.

1 JOHN 4:10

We love him, because he first loved us.

1 JOHN 4:19

Greater love has no one than this: to lay down one's life for one's friends.

JOHN 15:13 NIV

See what great love the Father has lavished on us, that we should be called children of God! And that is what we are! The reason the world does not know us is that it did not know him.

1 JOHN 3:1 NIV

Our love for God

The LORD preserveth all them that love him: but all the wicked will he destroy.

PSALM 145:20

I love them that love me; and those that seek me early shall find me.

PROVERBS 8:17

For the Father himself loveth you, because ye have loved me, and have believed that I came out from God.

JOHN 16:27

Know therefore that the LORD your God is God; he
is the faithful God, keeping his covenant of love to a
thousand generations of those who love him and keep his
commands.

DEUTERONOMY 7:9 NIV

Our love for each other

Love must be sincere. Hate what is evil; cling to what is
good. Be devoted to one another in brotherly love. Honor
one another above yourselves.

ROMANS 12:9–10 NIV

A new commandment I give unto you, That ye love one
another; as I have loved you, that ye also love one another.
By this shall all men know that ye are my disciples, if ye
have love one to another.

JOHN 13:34–35

Beloved, let us love one another: for love is of God; and
every one that loveth is born of God, and knoweth God.
He that loveth not knoweth not God; for God is love.

1 JOHN 4:7–8

Love is patient, love is kind. It does not envy, it does not
boast, it is not proud. It does not dishonor others, it is not
self-seeking, it is not easily angered, it keeps no record
of wrongs. Love does not delight in evil but rejoices with
the truth. It always protects, always trusts, always hopes,
always perseveres. Love never fails.

1 CORINTHIANS 13:4–8 NIV

Whoever claims to love God yet hates a brother or sister is a liar. For whoever does not love their brother and sister, whom have seen, cannot love God, whom they they have not seen.

1 JOHN 4:20 NIV

Q: When you hear the word "love," what's the first thing you think of? What's the second thing?

Loyalty

Def.: the state or quality of being loyal; devoted attachment and affection; steadfast in allegiance to a country, a cause, a person, or an ideal.

Friends are loyal. They are with you in good and bad times. They do not leave when the going gets rough or when you are rough. They are not just friends when you are in a good mood! This loyalty does not mean that they will cover your faults and worship you.

PAUL JEHLE
DATING VS. COURTSHIP

Then they would put their trust in God and would not forget his deeds but would keep his commands. They would not be like their ancestors—a stubborn and rebellious generation, whose hearts were not loyal to God, whose spirits were not faithful to him.

PSALM 78:7–8 NIV

Thou shalt have no other gods before me. Thou shalt not bow down thyself to them, nor serve them: for I the LORD thy God am a jealous God.

EXODUS 20:3, 5

If it be so, our God whom we serve is able to deliver us from the burning fiery furnace, and he will deliver us out of thine hand, O king. But if not, be it known unto thee, O king, that we will not serve thy gods, nor worship the golden image which thou hast set up.

Daniel 3:17-18

And Ruth said, Intreat me not to leave thee, or to return from following after thee: for whither thou goest, I will go; and where thou lodgest, I will lodge: thy people shall be my people, and thy God my God: Where thou diest, will I die, and there will I be buried: the LORD do so to me, and more also, if ought but death part thee and me.

Ruth 1:16-17

LORD, the God of our fathers Abraham, Isaac and Israel, keep these desires and thoughts in the hearts of your people forever, and keep their hearts loyal to you.

1 Chronicles 29:18 NIV

Q: Do you demonstrate the kind of loyalty to family and friends that you expect in return?

Lust

76% of women believe that participating in phone sex or cyber-sex is the same as committing adultery; only 41% of men believe the same.

Your flesh, creative and cool as it is, will invariably remind you of a dozen ways to rationalize around the wrong of your lust.

CHARLES SWINDOLL
MAN TO MAN

Ye have heard that it was said by them of old time, Thou shalt not commit adultery: But I say unto you, That whosoever looketh on a woman to lust after her hath committed adultery with her already in his heart.

MATTHEW 5:27–28

Flee also youthful lusts: but follow righteousness, faith, charity, peace, with them that call on the Lord out of a pure heart.

2 TIMOTHY 2:22

...that each of you should learn to control your own body in a way that is holy and honorable, not in passionate lust like the pagans, who do not know God.

1 THESSALONIANS 4:4–5 NIV

Do not lust in your heart after her beauty or let her captivate you with her eyes. Can a man scoop fire into his lap without his clothes being burned? Can a man walk on hot coals without his feet being scorched? So is he who sleeps with another man's wife; no one who touches her will go unpunished.

PROVERBS 6:25, 27–29 NIV

From whence come wars and fightings among you? come they not hence, even of your lusts that war in your members? Ye lust, and have not: ye kill, and desire to have, and cannot obtain: ye fight and war, yet ye have not, because ye ask not. Ye ask, and receive not, because ye ask amiss, that ye may consume it upon your lusts. Ye adulterers and adulteresses, know ye not that the friendship of the world is enmity with God? whosoever therefore will be a friend of the world is the enemy of God.

JAMES 4:1–4

Love not the world, neither the things that are in the world. If any man love the world, the love of the Father is not in him. For all that is in the world, the lust of the flesh, and the lust of the eyes, and the pride of life, is not of the Father, but is of the world. And the world passeth away, and the lust thereof: but he that doeth the will of God abideth for ever.

1 JOHN 2:15–17

As obedient children, do not conform to the evil desires you had when you lived in ignorance.

1 PETER 1:14 NIV

Remember all the commands of the LORD, that you may obey them and not prostitute yourselves by chasing after the lusts of your own hearts and eyes.

NUMBERS 15:39 NIV

This I say then, Walk in the Spirit, and ye shall not fulfil the lust of the flesh. For the flesh lusteth against the Spirit, and the Spirit against the flesh: and these are contrary the one to the other: so that ye cannot do the things that ye would.

GALATIANS 5:16–17

Q: Do you sincerely believe that lust itself is sin—or that only acting on lust is sin?

Marriage

I'd rather not rule the earth. I just want to marry the girl next door and live in the suburbs.

COMIC BOOK HERO DYNAMO

That moment when you kiss someone. . .and you realize that that person is the only person that you're supposed to kiss for the rest of your life.

FROM THE MOVIE NEVER BEEN KISSED

And the LORD God said, It is not good that the man should be alone; I will make him an help meet for him. And Adam said, This is now bone of my bones, and flesh of my flesh: she shall be called Woman, because she was taken out of Man. Therefore shall a man leave his father and his mother, and shall cleave unto his wife: and they shall be one flesh.

GENESIS 2:18, 23–24

Whoso findeth a wife findeth a good thing, and obtaineth favour of the LORD.

PROVERBS 18:22

Be ye not unequally yoked together with unbelievers: for what fellowship hath righteousness with unrighteousness? and what communion hath light with darkness?

2 CORINTHIANS 6:14

Submit to one another out of reverence for Christ. Wives, submit yourselves to your own husbands as you do to the Lord.

Ephesians 5:21–22 niv

Husbands, in the same way be considerate as you live with your wives, and treat them with respect as the weaker partner and as heirs with you of the gracious gift of life, so that nothing will hinder your prayers.

1 Peter 3:7 niv

Husbands, love your wives, even as Christ also loved the church, and gave himself for it.

Ephesians 5:25

However, each one of you also must love his wife as he loves himself, and the wife must respect her husband.

Ephesians 5:33 niv

The husband should fulfill his marital duty to his wife, and likewise the wife to her husband. The wife does not have authority over her own body but yields it to her husband. In the same way, the husband does not have authority over his own body but yields it to his wife. Do not deprive each other except perhaps by mutual consent and for a time, so that you may devote yourselves to prayer. Then come together again so that Satan will not tempt you because of your lack of self-control.

1 Corinthian 7:3–5 niv

Marriage is honourable in all, and the bed undefiled: but whoremongers and adulterers God will judge.

HEBREWS 13:4

Let thy fountain be blessed: and rejoice with the wife of thy youth. Let her be as the loving hind and pleasant roe; let her breasts satisfy thee at all times; and be thou ravished always with her love.

PROVERBS 5:18–19

Live joyfully with the wife whom thou lovest all the days of the life of thy vanity, which he hath given thee under the sun. . .for that is thy portion in this life, and in thy labour which thou takest under the sun.

ECCLESIASTES 9:9

Q: What percent of your marriage do you think will be romantic and fun? What percent will be hard work?

Miracles

% of teens who "definitely" believe in miracles
from God: 61

Being worshipers at the altar of science, we
don't like to believe miracles exist, but they do.
Things happen. We can't explain them, we can't
control them, but they *do* happen.

FROM THE TV SERIES *GREY'S ANATOMY*

You are the God who performs miracles; you display your
power among the peoples.

PSALM 77:14 NIV

Seek the LORD, and his strength: seek his face evermore.
Remember his marvellous works that he hath done; his
wonders, and the judgments of his mouth.

PSALM 105:4-5

And in that same hour he cured many of their infirmities
and plagues, and of evil spirits; and unto many that were
blind he gave sight. Then Jesus answering said unto them,
Go your way, and tell John what things ye have seen and
heard; how that the blind see, the lame walk, the lepers
are cleansed, the deaf hear, the dead are raised, to the
poor the gospel is preached.

LUKE 7:21-22

And he could there do no mighty work, save that he laid his hands upon a few sick folk, and healed them. And he marvelled because of their unbelief.

MARK 6:5–6

Jesus answered them, I told you, and ye believed not: the works that I do in my Father's name, they bear witness of me.

JOHN 10:25

But though he had done so many miracles before them, yet they believed not on him.

JOHN 12:37

"Do not believe me unless I do the works of my Father. But if I do them, even though you do not believe me, believe the works, that you may know and understand that the Father is in me, and I in the Father."

JOHN 10:37–38 NIV

And many of the people believed on him, and said, When Christ cometh, will he do more miracles than these which this man hath done?

JOHN 7:31

As the crowds increased, Jesus said, "This is a wicked generation. It asks for a sign, but none will be given it except the sign of Jonah. For as Jonah was a sign to the Ninevites, so also will the Son of Man be to this generation."

LUKE 11:29–30 NIV

And many other signs truly did Jesus in the presence of his disciples, which are not written in this book: But these are written, that ye might believe that Jesus is the Christ, the Son of God; and that believing ye might have life through his name.

JOHN 20:30–31

Believe me that I am in the Father, and the Father in me: or else believe me for the very works' sake. Verily, verily, I say unto you, He that believeth on me, the works that I do shall he do also; and greater works than these shall he do; because I go unto my Father.

JOHN 14:11–12

Everyone was filled with awe at the many wonders and signs performed by the apostles.

ACTS 2:43 NIV

For the Jews require a sign, and the Greeks seek after wisdom: But we preach Christ crucified, unto the Jews a stumblingblock, and unto the Greeks foolishness; But unto them which are called, both Jews and Greeks, Christ the power of God, and the wisdom of God.

1 CORINTHIANS 1:22–24

How shall we escape if we ignore so great a salvation? This salvation, which was first announced by the Lord, was confirmed to us by those who heard him. God also testified to it by signs, wonders and various miracles, and by gifts of the Holy Spirit distributed according to his will.

HEBREWS 2:3–4 NIV

Q: Can you think of any miracles that have happened in your life or in your parents' lives?

Money

In a 2011 survey of teens 18 years old:
- 74% say they have been taught how to use a credit card responsibly
- 39% say they're "knowledgeable about how to manage a credit card"
- 32% say they know "how credit card interest and fees work"

You're not your job. You're not how much money you have in the bank. You're not the car you drive. You're not the contents of your wallet.

FROM THE MOVIE *Fight Club*

Whoever loves money never has money enough; whoever loves wealth is never satisfied with their income.

ECCLESIASTES 5:10 NIV

"No one can serve two masters. Either you will hate the one and love the other, or you will be devoted to the one and despise the other. You cannot serve both God and money."

LUKE 16:13 NIV

For the love of money is the root of all evil: which while some coveted after, they have erred from the faith, and pierced themselves through with many sorrows.

1 TIMOTHY 6:10

A little that a righteous man hath is better than the riches of many wicked.

PSALM 37:16

Charge them that are rich in this world, that they be not highminded, nor trust in uncertain riches, but in the living God, who giveth us richly all things to enjoy.

1 TIMOTHY 6:17

He that is faithful in that which is least is faithful also in much: and he that is unjust in the least is unjust also in much. If therefore ye have not been faithful in the unrighteous mammon, who will commit to your trust the true riches?

LUKE 16:10–11

Ho, every one that thirsteth, come ye to the waters, and he that hath no money; come ye, buy, and eat; yea, come, buy wine and milk without money and without price. Wherefore do ye spend money for that which is not bread? and your labour for that which satisfieth not? hearken diligently unto me, and eat ye that which is good, and let your soul delight itself in fatness.

ISAIAH 55:1–2

But my God shall supply all your need according to his riches in glory by Christ Jesus.

PHILIPPIANS 4:19

Better is little with the fear of the LORD than great treasure and trouble therewith.

PROVERBS 15:16

He that trusteth in his riches shall fall; but the righteous shall flourish as a branch.

PROVERBS 11:28

Whoso mocketh the poor reproacheth his Maker: and he that is glad at calamities shall not be unpunished.

PROVERBS 17:5

Not that I speak in respect of want: for I have learned, in whatsoever state I am, therewith to be content. I know both how to be abased, and I know how to abound: every where and in all things I am instructed both to be full and to be hungry, both to abound and to suffer need.

PHILIPPIANS 4:11–12

Keep your lives free from the love of money and be content with what you have, because God has said, "Never will I leave you; never will I forsake you."

HEBREWS 13:5 NIV

His lord said unto him, Well done, thou good and faithful servant: thou hast been faithful over a few things, I will make thee ruler over many things: enter thou into the joy of thy lord.

MATTHEW 25:21

Wealth gotten by vanity shall be diminished: but he that gathereth by labour shall increase.

PROVERBS 13:11

Q: How knowledgeable are you about money—its value, its responsible use, and its place in your life?

Music

You know, you're much too tense. You're a young man. You need to relax, learn to take some joy in your work. Do you like music?

FROM THE MOVIE MEN IN BLACK

The aim and final end of all music should be none other than the glory of God and the refreshment of the soul.

JOHANN SEBASTIAN BACH

"Hear this, you kings! Listen, you rulers! I, even I, will sing to the LORD; I will praise the LORD, the God of Israel, in song."

JUDGES 5:3 NIV

Praise him with the sound of the trumpet: praise him with the psaltery and harp. Praise him with the timbrel and dance: praise him with stringed instruments and organs. Praise him upon the loud cymbals: praise him upon the high sounding cymbals. Let every thing that hath breath praise the LORD. Praise ye the LORD.

PSALM 150:3–6

Let them praise his name in the dance: let them sing praises unto him with the timbrel and harp.

PSALM 149:3

And at the dedication of the wall of Jerusalem they sought the Levites. . .to bring them to Jerusalem, to keep the dedication with gladness, both with thanksgivings, and with singing, with cymbals, psalteries, and with harps.

NEHEMIAH 12:27

And now shall mine head be lifted up above mine enemies round about me: therefore will I offer in his tabernacle sacrifices of joy; I will sing, yea, I will sing praises unto the LORD.

PSALM 27:6

Praise the LORD with harp: sing unto him with the psaltery and an instrument of ten strings. Sing unto him a new song; play skilfully with a loud noise.

PSALM 33:2–3

Let the words of my mouth, and the meditation of my heart, be acceptable in thy sight, O LORD, my strength, and my redeemer.

PSALM 19:14

Make a joyful noise unto the LORD, all the earth: make a loud noise, and rejoice, and sing praise.

PSALM 98:4

Speaking to one another with psalms, hymns, and songs from the Spirit. Sing and make music from your heart to the Lord, always giving thanks to God the Father for everything, in the name of our Lord Jesus Christ.

EPHESIANS 5:19–20 NIV

Q: What kind of music do you enjoy most of the time? How much does worship music move you?

Obedience

Def.: *1.* the act or practice of obeying; *2.* submission to another's rule or authority; *3.* compliance with a law or command

Obedience, when it flows out of a genuine love for Jesus Christ, is never wasted and never regretted.

LESLIE LUDY
SACRED SINGLENESS

See, I am setting before you today a blessing and a curse—the blessing if you obey the commands of the LORD your God that I am giving you today; the curse if you disobey the commands of the LORD your God and turn from the way that I command you today by following other gods, which you have not known.

DEUTERONOMY 11:26–28 NIV

And Samuel said, Hath the LORD as great delight in burnt offerings and sacrifices, as in obeying the voice of the LORD? Behold, to obey is better than sacrifice, and to hearken than the fat of rams.

1 SAMUEL 15:22

For this is the love of God, that we keep his commandments: and his commandments are not grievous.

1 JOHN 5:3

Thou shalt therefore obey the voice of the LORD thy God, and do his commandments and his statutes, which I command thee this day.

DEUTERONOMY 27:10

If ye love me, keep my commandments. Jesus answered and said unto him, If a man love me, he will keep my words: and my Father will love him, and we will come unto him, and make our abode with him.

JOHN 14:15, 23

And he went a little farther, and fell on his face, and prayed, saying, O my Father, if it be possible, let this cup pass from me: nevertheless not as I will, but as thou wilt.

MATTHEW 26:39

And hereby we do know that we know him, if we keep his commandments. He that saith, I know him, and keepeth not his commandments, is a liar, and the truth is not in him.

1 JOHN 2:3–4

Not every one that saith unto me, Lord, Lord, shall enter into the kingdom of heaven; but he that doeth the will of my Father which is in heaven.

MATTHEW 7:21

Q: How obedient are you to your parents? To your teachers? To your boss? To God?

The Occult

Data:
- 73% of American teens are seriously exploring the occult
- 1 in 12 have actually cast spells or made magical potions
- 29% of Christian teens think Ouija boards are harmless

Medium Oda Mae Brown: Julio's coming towards us. I see him! He's coming! He's there! He's dressed in a black suit.
Rosa Santiago: [long pause] Black suit?
Oda Mae Brown: [pause] Could be blue!

FROM THE MOVIE *GHOST*

Let no one be found among you who sacrifices their son or daughter in the fire, who practices divination or sorcery, interprets omens, engages in witchcraft, or casts spells, or who is a medium or spiritist or who consults the dead. Anyone who does these things is detestable to the LORD; because of these same detestable practices the LORD your God will drive out those nations before you.

DEUTERONOMY 18:10–12 NIV

Saul died because he was unfaithful to the LORD; he did not keep the word of the LORD and even consulted a medium for guidance, and did not inquire of the LORD. So the LORD put him to death and turned the kingdom over to David son of Jesse.

1 CHRONICLES 10:13–14 NIV

"But the cowardly, the unbelieving, the vile, the murderers, the sexually immoral, those who practice magic arts, the idolaters and all liars—they will be consigned to the fiery lake of burning sulfur. This is the second death."

REVELATION 21:8 NIV

And the soul that turneth after such as have familiar spirits, and after wizards, to go a whoring after them, I will even set my face against that soul, and will cut him off from among his people.

LEVITICUS 20:6

Therefore shall evil come upon thee; thou shalt not know from whence it riseth: and mischief shall fall upon thee; thou shalt not be able to put it off: and desolation shall come upon thee suddenly, which thou shalt not know. Stand now with thine enchantments, and with the multitude of thy sorceries, wherein thou hast laboured from thy youth. . . . Thou art wearied in the multitude of thy counsels. Let now the astrologers, the stargazers, the monthly prognosticators, stand up, and save thee from these things that shall come upon thee. Behold, they shall be as stubble; the fire shall burn them; they shall not deliver themselves from the power of the flame. . .none shall save thee.

ISAIAH 47:11–15

Greater is he that is in you, than he that is in the world.

1 JOHN 4:4

Giving thanks unto the Father, which hath made us meet to be partakers of the inheritance of the saints in light: Who hath delivered us from the power of darkness, and hath translated us into the kingdom of his dear Son: In whom we have redemption through his blood, even the forgiveness of sins.

COLOSSIANS 1:12–14

Q: Why do you think the Bible speaks against the occult? Have you dabbled in it?

Parents

You can't judge your father by his actions and yourself by your intentions. It just doesn't work that way.

FROM THE MOVIE *FACING THE GIANTS*

Nate Saint: Do you know how far away the sun is?
Young Steve Saint: 93 million miles.
Nate Saint: Do you know that that's just a fraction of how much I love you?

FROM THE MOVIE *END OF THE SPEAR*

Whoso curseth his father or his mother, his lamp shall be put out in obscure darkness.

PROVERBS 20:20

Whoever robs their father and drives out their mother is a child who brings shame and disgrace.

PROVERBS 19:26 NIV

Whoso robbeth his father or his mother, and saith, It is no transgression; the same is the companion of a destroyer.

PROVERBS 28:24

"Each of you must respect your mother and father."

LEVITICUS 19:3 NIV

The father of the righteous shall greatly rejoice: and he that begetteth a wise child shall have joy of him.

PROVERBS 23:24

Thou knowest the commandments, Do not commit adultery, Do not kill, Do not steal, Do not bear false witness, Honour thy father and thy mother.

LUKE 18:20

Children, obey your parents in all things: for this is well pleasing unto the Lord

COLOSSIANS 3:20

Children, obey your parents in the Lord, for this is right. "Honor your father and mother"—which is the first commandment with a promise—"so that it may go well with you and that you may enjoy long life on the earth."

EPHESIANS 6:1–3 NIV

Q: Despite sometimes being frustrated with them, have you learned to appreciate your parents?

Patience

Def.: the capacity to accept delay, trouble, or suffering without getting angry or upset; tolerant endurance of hardship, provocation, or pain; the ability for calm, composed waiting.

God sometimes does His work with gentle drizzle, not storms. Drip. Drip. Drip.

FROM THE MOVIE *AMAZING GRACE*

Rest in the LORD, and wait patiently for him: fret not thyself because of him who prospereth in his way, because of the man who bringeth wicked devices to pass.

PSALM 37:7

Be patient toward all men. See that none render evil for evil unto any man; but ever follow that which is good, both among yourselves, and to all men.

1 THESSALONIANS 5:14–15

But the fruit of the Spirit is love, joy, peace, forbearance. . . .

GALATIANS 5:22 NIV

But we glory in tribulations also: knowing that tribulation worketh patience; and patience, experience; and experience, hope.

ROMANS 5:3–4

The patient in spirit is better than the proud in spirit.

ECCLESIASTES 7:8

Love is patient, love is kind. . . . It is not easily angered.

1 CORINTHIANS 13:4–5 NIV

And let us not be weary in well doing: for in due season we shall reap, if we faint not.

GALATIANS 6:9

Be patient, then, brothers and sisters, until the Lord's coming. See how the farmer waits for the land to yield its valuable crop, patiently waiting for the autumn and spring rains. You too, be patient and stand firm, because the Lord's coming is near.

JAMES 5:7–8 NIV

For ye have need of patience, that, after ye have done the will of God, ye might receive the promise.

HEBREWS 10:36

Q: On a scale of 1 to 10, when things go badly wrong, how patient are you? What are the chances of you melting down?

Peace

Judah Ben-Hur: [bitterly] Peace! Love and peace. Do you think I don't long for them as you do? Where do you see them?
Esther: If you had heard this man from Nazareth. . .

FROM THE MOVIE BEN-HUR

The most striking characteristic of men and women who are doing God's work His way is their lack of stress. Believers who are walking in the Spirit are going to experience peace.

CHARLES STANLEY
THE WONDERFUL SPIRIT-FILLED LIFE

Peace I leave with you, my peace I give unto you: not as the world giveth, give I unto you. Let not your heart be troubled, neither let it be afraid.

JOHN 14:27

Therefore being justified by faith, we have peace with God through our Lord Jesus Christ.

ROMANS 5:1

Depart from evil, and do good; seek peace, and pursue it.

PSALM 34:14

And, having made peace through the blood of his cross, by him to reconcile all things unto himself; by him, I say, whether they be things in earth, or things in heaven.

Colossians 1:20

Now the God of hope fill you with all joy and peace in believing, that ye may abound in hope, through the power of the Holy Ghost.

Romans 15:13

And the peace of God, which transcends all understanding, will guard your hearts and your minds in Christ Jesus.

Philippians 4:7 niv

And we know that all things work together for good to them that love God, to them who are the called according to his purpose.

Romans 8:28

Follow peace with all men, and holiness, without which no man shall see the Lord.

Hebrews 12:14

Thou wilt keep him in perfect peace, whose mind is stayed on thee: because he trusteth in thee.

Isaiah 26:3

"I have told you these things, so that in me you may have peace. In this world you will have trouble. But take heart! I have overcome the world."

John 16:33 niv

Q: Do you have peace or are you often troubled? What kinds of things stress you?

Peer Pressure

- 70% of teens who smoke started due to peer pressure
- 33% of teen boys are pressured by friends to have sex
- 23% of teen girls are pressured by friends to have sex

We all have a great need of acceptance, but you must trust that your beliefs are unique, your own, even though others may think them odd or unpopular.

FROM THE MOVIE *DEAD POETS SOCIETY*

Therefore, I urge you, brothers and sisters, in view of God's mercy, to offer your bodies as a living sacrifice, holy and pleasing to God—this is your true and proper worship. Do not conform to the pattern of this world, but be transformed by the renewing of your mind. Then you will be able to test and approve what God's will is—his good, pleasing and perfect will.

ROMANS 12:1–2 NIV

Walk worthy of God, who hath called you unto his kingdom and glory

1 THESSALONIANS 2:12

Therefore, "Come out from them and be separate, says the Lord. Touch no unclean thing, and I will receive you." And, "I will be a Father to you, and you will be my sons and daughters, says the Lord Almighty."

2 CORINTHIANS 6:17–18 NIV

As obedient children, not fashioning yourselves according to the former lusts in your ignorance: But as he which hath called you is holy, so be ye holy in all manner of conversation; Because it is written, Be ye holy; for I am holy.

1 PETER 1:14–16

Since we have these promises, dear friends, let us purify ourselves from everything that contaminates body and spirit, perfecting holiness out of reverence for God.

2 CORINTHIANS 7:1 NIV

Prove all things; hold fast that which is good. Abstain from all appearance of evil.

1 THESSALONIANS 5:21–22

For God hath not called us unto uncleanness, but unto holiness.

1 THESSALONIANS 4:7

But in your hearts revere Christ as Lord. Always be prepared to give an answer to everyone who asks you to give the reason for the hope that you have. But do this with gentleness and respect, keeping a clear conscience, so that those who speak maliciously against your good behavior in Christ may be ashamed of their slander.

1 PETER 3:15–16 NIV

Q: Do your friends pressure you to do immoral or illegal things? Have you considered finding new friends?

Persecution

Def.: 1. the act of persecuting; subjecting someone to hostility or ill-treatment because of their religious beliefs, race, etc; 2. to harass, oppress, persistently annoy.

Unfortunately, many of the young people who attend public schools and universities in America today are being persecuted for their profession of faith in Christ.

JUDGE ROY MOORE

"Blessed are those who are persecuted because of righteousness, for theirs is the kingdom of heaven. Blessed are you when people insult you, persecute you and falsely say all kinds of evil against you because of me. Rejoice and be glad, because great is your reward in heaven, for in the same way they persecuted the prophets who were before you."

MATTHEW 5:10–12 NIV

And ye shall be hated of all men for my name's sake: but he that endureth to the end shall be saved.

MATTHEW 10:22

All thy commandments are faithful: they persecute me wrongfully; help thou me.

PSALM 119:86

Remember the word that I said unto you, The servant is not greater than his lord. If they have persecuted me, they will also persecute you; if they have kept my saying, they will keep yours also.

JOHN 15:20

Bless them which persecute you: bless, and curse not.

ROMANS 12:14

Yea, and all that will live godly in Christ Jesus shall suffer persecution.

2 TIMOTHY 3:12

When we are cursed, we bless; when we are persecuted, we endure it; when we are slandered, we answer kindly.

1 CORINTHIANS 4:12–13 NIV

Q: Have you ever taken a public stand for your faith in Jesus Christ? Were you persecuted as a result?

Pornography

% of Internet search requests seeking pornographic images: 25
# of Americans who use the Internet to gratify their sexual desires: 40,000,000

When you get the personality, you don't need the nudity.

MAE WEST

Know ye not that the unrighteous shall not inherit the kingdom of God? Be not deceived: neither fornicators, nor idolaters, nor adulterers, nor effeminate, nor abusers of themselves with mankind, nor thieves, nor covetous, nor drunkards, nor revilers, nor extortioners, shall inherit the kingdom of God.

1 CORINTHIANS 6:9–10

So I tell you this, and insist on it in the Lord, that you must no longer live as the Gentiles do, in the futility of their thinking. They are darkened in their understanding and separated from the life of God because of the ignorance that is in them due to the hardening of their hearts. Having lost all sensitivity, they have given themselves over to sensuality so as to indulge in every kind of impurity, and they are full of greed. That, however, is not the way of life you learned.

EPHESIANS 4:17–20 NIV

Let this mind be in you, which was also in Christ Jesus.

PHILIPPIANS 2:5

And have no fellowship with the unfruitful works of darkness, but rather reprove them. For it is a shame even to speak of those things which are done of them in secret.

EPHESIANS 5:11–12

Finally, brethren, whatsoever things are true, whatsoever things are honest, whatsoever things are just, whatsoever things are pure, whatsoever things are lovely, whatsoever things are of good report; if there be any virtue, and if there be any praise, think on these things.

PHILIPPIANS 4:8

Q: What is your position on viewing soft-core porn? What about lingering over swimsuit or underwear ads?

Prayer

That's not why I pray, Harry. I pray because I can't help myself. I pray because I'm helpless. I pray because the need flows out of me all the time, waking and sleeping.

FROM THE MOVIE *SHADOWLANDS*

Prayer is a declaration of our dependence on God. It isn't something mechanical you do; it is somewhere you go to meet Someone you know.

JILL BRISCOE
THE NEW NORMAL

The eyes of the LORD are on the righteous and his ears are attentive to their cry. . . . The righteous cry out, and the LORD hears them; he delivers them from all their troubles. The LORD is close to the brokenhearted and saves those who are crushed in spirit.

PSALM 34:15, 17–18 NIV

I will offer to thee the sacrifice of thanksgiving, and will call upon the name of the LORD.

PSALM 116:17

And all things, whatsoever ye shall ask in prayer, believing, ye shall receive.

MATTHEW 21:22

And when thou prayest, thou shalt not be as the hypocrites are: for they love to pray standing in the synagogues and in the corners of the streets, that they may be seen of men. Verily I say unto you, They have their reward. But thou, when thou prayest, enter into thy closet, and when thou hast shut thy door, pray to thy Father which is in secret; and thy Father which seeth in secret shall reward thee openly.

MATTHEW 6:5-6

After this manner therefore pray ye: Our Father which art in heaven, Hallowed be thy name. Thy kingdom come, Thy will be done in earth, as it is in heaven. Give us this day our daily bread. And forgive us our debts, as we forgive our debtors. And lead us not into temptation, but deliver us from evil: For thine is the kingdom, and the power, and the glory, for ever. Amen.

MATTHEW 6:9-13

Ask, and it shall be given you; seek, and ye shall find; knock, and it shall be opened unto you: For every one that asketh receiveth; and he that seeketh findeth; and to him that knocketh it shall be opened.

MATTHEW 7:7-8

Therefore I say unto you, What things soever ye desire, when ye pray, believe that ye receive them, and ye shall have them. And when ye stand praying, forgive, if ye have ought against any: that your Father also which is in heaven may forgive you your trespasses.

MARK 11:24-25

And whatsoever ye shall ask in my name, that will I do, that the Father may be glorified in the Son. If ye shall ask any thing in my name, I will do it.

JOHN 14:13-14

If ye abide in me, and my words abide in you, ye shall ask what ye will, and it shall be done unto you.

JOHN 15:7

Is any among you afflicted? let him pray. Is any merry? let him sing psalms. Confess your faults one to another, and pray one for another, that ye may be healed. The effectual fervent prayer of a righteous man availeth much.

JAMES 5:13, 16

Pray without ceasing.

1 THESSALONIANS 5:17

Praying always with all prayer and supplication in the Spirit, and watching thereunto with all perseverance and supplication for all saints.

EPHESIANS 6:18

I exhort therefore, that, first of all, supplications, prayers, intercessions, and giving of thanks, be made for all men.

1 TIMOTHY 2:1

Be careful for nothing; but in every thing by prayer and supplication with thanksgiving let your requests be made known unto God.

PHILIPPIANS 4:6

If I regard iniquity in my heart, the Lord will not hear me.

PSALM 66:18

The sacrifice of the wicked is an abomination to the LORD: but the prayer of the upright is his delight.

PROVERBS 15:8

Q: What do you spend most of your time praying about? How many of your prayers are answered?

Pride

Scratch any sin and just below the surface you'll find pride.

FROM THE MOVIE *THE ENCOUNTER*

A person may be proud without being vain. Pride relates more to our opinion of ourselves; vanity, to what we would have others think of us.

JANE AUSTEN

For all that is in the world, the lust of the flesh, and the lust of the eyes, and the pride of life, is not of the Father, but is of the world.

1 JOHN 2:16

God resisteth the proud, but giveth grace unto the humble.

JAMES 4:6

For I say, through the grace given unto me, to every man that is among you, not to think of himself more highly than he ought to think.

ROMANS 12:3

When pride cometh, then cometh shame: but with the lowly is wisdom.

PROVERBS 11:2

Every one that is proud in heart is an abomination to the LORD: though hand join in hand, he shall not be unpunished.

PROVERBS 16:5

An high look, and a proud heart, and the plowing of the wicked, is sin.

PROVERBS 21:4

Likewise, ye younger, submit yourselves unto the elder. Yea, all of you be subject one to another, and be clothed with humility: for God resisteth the proud, and giveth grace to the humble.

1 PETER 5:5

Q: What's the difference between "taking pride" in your work, and being proud?

Prophecy

- In a 2002 survey, 59% of Americans believed that the events in the Book of Revelation will occur in the future.
- In a 2010 poll, 65% of evangelical leaders believed that Jesus will return and reign on earth.

Today as never before, we are beginning to see signs of our Lord's impending return.

DAVID JEREMIAH
WHAT IN THE WORLD IS GOING ON?

We have also a more sure word of prophecy; whereunto ye do well that ye take heed. . . . Knowing this first, that no prophecy of the scripture is of any private interpretation. For the prophecy came not in old time by the will of man: but holy men of God spake as they were moved by the Holy Ghost.

2 PETER 1:19–21

And then shall appear the sign of the Son of man in heaven: and then shall all the tribes of the earth mourn, and they shall see the Son of man coming in the clouds of heaven with power and great glory.

MATTHEW 24:30

We which are alive and remain unto the coming of the Lord shall not prevent them which are asleep. For the Lord himself shall descend from heaven with a shout, with the voice of the archangel, and with the trump of God: and the dead in Christ shall rise first: Then we which are alive and remain shall be caught up together with them in the clouds, to meet the Lord in the air: and so shall we ever be with the Lord. Wherefore comfort one another with these words.

1 THESSALONIANS 4:15–18

I saw in the night visions, and, behold, one like the Son of man came with the clouds of heaven, and came to the Ancient of days, and they brought him near before him. And there was given him dominion, and glory, and a kingdom, that all people, nations, and languages, should serve him: his dominion is an everlasting dominion, which shall not pass away, and his kingdom that which shall not be destroyed.

DANIEL 7:13–14

Behold, he cometh with clouds; and every eye shall see him, and they also which pierced him: and all kindreds of the earth shall wail because of him. Even so, Amen.

REVELATION 1:7

Whosoever therefore shall be ashamed of me and of my words in this adulterous and sinful generation; of him also shall the Son of man be ashamed, when he cometh in the glory of his Father with the holy angels.

MARK 8:38

But the day of the Lord will come as a thief in the night; in the which the heavens shall pass away with a great noise, and the elements shall melt with fervent heat, the earth also and the works that are therein shall be burned up. Seeing then that all these things shall be dissolved, what manner of persons ought ye to be in all holy conversation and godliness, Looking for and hasting unto the coming of the day of God. . . ? Nevertheless we, according to his promise, look for new heavens and a new earth, wherein dwelleth righteousness.

2 PETER 3:10–13

Q: Do you believe that we're living in the end times? How does this view affect your daily life?

Punishment

Men are punished by God for their sins often visibly, always secretly, either in this life or after death.

St. Augustine
The City of God

"Your wickedness will punish you; your backsliding will rebuke you. Consider then and realize how evil and bitter it is for you when you forsake the Lord your God and have no awe of me," declares the Lord, the Lord Almighty.

Jeremiah 2:19 NIV

For if the word spoken by angels was stedfast, and every transgression and disobedience received a just recompence of reward; How shall we escape, if we neglect so great salvation. . . .

Hebrews 2:2–3

He that despised Moses' law died without mercy under two or three witnesses: Of how much sorer punishment, suppose ye, shall he be thought worthy, who hath trodden under foot the Son of God, and hath counted the blood of the covenant, wherewith he was sanctified, an unholy thing, and hath done despite unto the Spirit of grace? It is a fearful thing to fall into the hands of the living God.

Hebrews 10:28–29, 31

The Lord Jesus shall be revealed from heaven with his mighty angels, In flaming fire taking vengeance on them that know not God, and that obey not the gospel of our Lord Jesus Christ.

2 THESSALONIANS 1:7–8

Q: Do you seek to do good because you love God, or because you fear the consequences if you don't?

Respect

Why can't you give me the respect that I'm entitled to? Why can't you treat me like I would be treated by any stranger on the street?

FROM THE MOVIE *MOMMIE DEAREST*

Respect for ourselves guides our morals; respect for others guides our manners.

LAURENCE STERNE

Honour all men. Love the brotherhood. Fear God. Honour the king.

1 PETER 2:17

"Stand up in the presence of the aged, show respect for the elderly and revere your God. I am the LORD."

LEVITICUS 19:32 NIV

That all men should honour the Son, even as they honour the Father. He that honoureth not the Son honoureth not the Father which hath sent him.

JOHN 5:23

But now the LORD declares. . . "Those who honor me I will honor, but those who despise me will be disdained."

1 SAMUEL 2:30 NIV

The wife must respect her husband.

EPHESIANS 5:33 NIV

Husbands, in the same way be considerate as you live with
your wives, and treat them with respect as the weaker
partner and as heirs with you of the gracious gift of life, so
that nothing will hinder your prayers.

1 PETER 3:7 NIV

Honour thy father and thy mother: that thy days may be
long upon the land which the LORD thy God giveth thee.

EXODUS 20:12

Q: How difficult or how easy do you find it to
treat others with courtesy and respect?

Restitution

Sally Brown: You blockhead! You kept me up all night waiting for the Great Pumpkin, and all that came was a beagle! I didn't get a chance to go out for tricks or treats. *You owe me restitution!*

FROM *IT'S THE GREAT PUMPKIN, CHARLIE BROWN*

"Anyone who steals must certainly make restitution, but if they have nothing, they must be sold to pay for their theft. If the stolen animal is found alive in their possession— whether ox or donkey or sheep—they must pay back double."

EXODUS 22:3–4 NIV

Men do not despise a thief, if he steal to satisfy his soul when he is hungry; But if he be found, he shall restore sevenfold; he shall give all the substance of his house.

PROVERBS 6:30–31

"If anyone sins and is unfaithful to the LORD by deceiving a neighbor about something entrusted to them or left in their care or about something stolen, or if they cheat their neighbor. . .or whatever it was they swore falsely about. They must make restitution in full, add a fifth of the value to it and give it all to the owner on the day they present their guilt offering."

LEVITICUS 6:2, 5 NIV

And Zacchaeus stood, and said unto the Lord: Behold, Lord, the half of my goods I give to the poor; and if I have taken any thing from any man by false accusation, I restore him fourfold. And Jesus said unto him, This day is salvation come to this house, forsomuch as he also is a son of Abraham.

LUKE 19:8–9

Q: If you have wronged or offended someone have you done what you can to make things right?

Resurrection

The body sluggish, aged, cold, the embers left from earlier fires shall duly flame again.

FROM THE MOVIE THE NOTEBOOK

The resurrection of our Saviour Christ, in the preaching of the gospel, raises earthquakes in the world now, as when Christ arose out of the sepulchre bodily.

MARTIN LUTHER
TABLE TALK

O LORD, thou hast brought up my soul from the grave: thou hast kept me alive, that I should not go down to the pit. But thou, O LORD, be merciful unto me, and raise me up, that I may requite them.

PSALM 30:3, 41:10

And he saith unto them, Be not affrighted: Ye seek Jesus of Nazareth, which was crucified: he is risen; he is not here: behold the place where they laid him. But go your way, tell his disciples and Peter that he goeth before you into Galilee: there shall ye see him, as he said unto you.

MARK 16:6–7

Yet a little while, and the world seeth me no more; but ye see me: because I live, ye shall live also.

JOHN 14:19

Christ died for our sins according to the scriptures; And that he was buried, and that he rose again the third day according to the scriptures: And that he was seen of Cephas, then of the twelve: After that, he was seen of above five hundred brethren at once; of whom the greater part remain unto this present, but some are fallen asleep. After that, he was seen of James; then of all the apostles. And last of all he was seen of me also.

1 CORINTHIANS 15:3–8

And if Christ be not risen, then is our preaching vain, and your faith is also vain. And if Christ be not raised, your faith is vain; ye are yet in your sins. If in this life only we have hope in Christ, we are of all men most miserable. But now is Christ risen from the dead, and become the firstfruits of them that slept.

1 CORINTHIANS 15:14, 17, 19–20

Jesus said unto her, I am the resurrection, and the life: he that believeth in me, though he were dead, yet shall he live: And whosoever liveth and believeth in me shall never die. Believest thou this?

JOHN 11:25–26

And with great power gave the apostles witness of the resurrection of the Lord Jesus: and great grace was upon them all.

ACTS 4:33

Q: Do you believe that Jesus rose from the dead? What hope does this give you?

Revenge

Def.: inflicting hurt or harm on someone in return for a wrong suffered at their hands;to punish for an insult or injury; a.k.a. retaliation, payback, and getting even.

Retribution has no place in the life of any Christian.

JO BERRY

BELOVED UNBELIEVER

Dearly beloved, avenge not yourselves, but rather give place unto wrath: for it is written, Vengeance is mine; I will repay, saith the Lord.

ROMANS 12:19

Do not gloat when your enemy falls; when they stumble, do not let your heart rejoice.

PROVERBS 24:17 NIV

For we know him who said, "It is mine to avenge; I will repay," and again, "The Lord will judge his people." It is a dreadful thing to fall into the hands of the living God.

HEBREWS 10:30–31 NIV

"For if you forgive other people when they sin against you, your heavenly Father will also forgive you."

MATTHEW 6:14 NIV

"Do not seek revenge or bear a grudge against anyone among your people, but love your neighbor as yourself. I am the LORD."

LEVITICUS 19:18 NIV

"You have heard that it was said, 'Eye for eye, and tooth for tooth.' But I tell you, do not resist an evil person. If anyone slaps you on the right cheek, turn to them the other cheek also. And if anyone wants to sue you and take your shirt, hand over your coat as well. If anyone forces you to go one mile, go with them two miles."

MATTHEW 5:38-41 NIV

"It is mine to avenge; I will repay. In due time their foot will slip; their day of disaster is near and their doom rushes upon them."

DEUTERONOMY 32:35 NIV

I will make mine arrows drunk with blood, and my sword shall devour flesh; and that with the blood of the slain and of the captives, from the beginning of revenges upon the enemy.

DEUTERONOMY 32:42

See that none render evil for evil unto any man; but ever follow that which is good, both among yourselves, and to all men.

1 THESSALONIANS 5:15

Q: Do you ever ignore Jesus' commands against revenge, and pay someone back for hurting you?

Salvation

John Newton: Though I have lost my memory, two things I know. I am a great sinner and Christ is a great Savior.

FROM THE MOVIE AMAZING GRACE

When God brings us to salvation, the most remarkable thing we see is that he transforms our hungers. He changes not just what we do but what we want to do.

RAVI ZACHARIAS
THE GRAND WEAVER

The LORD is my strength and song, and he is become my salvation: he is my God. . .and I will exalt him.

EXODUS 15:2

And say ye, Save us, O God of our salvation, and gather us together, and deliver us from the heathen, that we may give thanks to thy holy name, and glory in thy praise.

1 CHRONICLES 16:35

Nevertheless he saved them for his name's sake, that he might make his mighty power to be known.

PSALM 106:8

And as Moses lifted up the serpent in the wilderness, even so must the Son of man be lifted up: That whosoever believeth in him should not perish, but have eternal life.

JOHN 3:14–15

Seek ye the LORD while he may be found, call ye upon him while he is near.

ISAIAH 55:6

To day if ye will hear his voice, Harden not your hearts, as in the provocation, in the day of temptation in the wilderness.

HEBREWS 3:7–8

Therefore if any man be in Christ, he is a new creature: old things are passed away; behold, all things are become new.

2 CORINTHIANS 5:17

"Salvation belongs to our God, who sits on the throne, and to the Lamb."

REVELATION 7:10 NIV

"Here I am! I stand at the door and knock. If anyone hears my voice and opens the door, I will come in and eat with that person, and they with me. To the one who is victorious, I will give the right to sit with me on my throne, just as I was victorious and sat down with my Father on his throne."

REVELATION 3:20–21 NIV

Jesus stood and cried, saying, If any man thirst, let him come unto me, and drink. He that believeth on me, as the scripture hath said, out of his belly shall flow rivers of living water.

JOHN 7:37–38

Q: Can you name three different reasons why God saved you?

Satan

- 82% of Americans believe in God
- 62% of Americans believe in the devil and hell
- 40% of Christians believe that the devil is not a living being, but merely a symbol of evil

Satan is not a metaphor for evil. He is a powerful angel who committed treason against his Creator and convinced a third of the angels to rebel along with him.

CHIP INGRAM
THE INVISIBLE WAR

Thou art the anointed cherub that covereth; and I have set thee so: thou wast upon the holy mountain of God; thou hast walked up and down in the midst of the stones of fire. Thou wast perfect in thy ways from the day that thou wast created, till iniquity was found in thee.

EZEKIEL 28:14–15

Ye are of your father the devil, and the lusts of your father ye will do. He was a murderer from the beginning, and abode not in the truth, because there is no truth in him. When he speaketh a lie, he speaketh of his own: for he is a liar, and the father of it.

JOHN 8:44

242

How art thou fallen from heaven, O Lucifer, son of the morning! how art thou cut down to the ground, which didst weaken the nations! For thou hast said in thine heart, I will ascend into heaven, I will exalt my throne above the stars of God. . . . I will be like the most High. Yet thou shalt be brought down to hell, to the sides of the pit. They that see thee shall narrowly look upon thee, and consider thee, saying, Is this the man that made the earth to tremble, that did shake kingdoms.

ISAIAH 14:12–16

Be sober, be vigilant; because your adversary the devil, as a roaring lion, walketh about, seeking whom he may devour.

1 PETER 5:8

But if our gospel be hid, it is hid to them that are lost: In whom the god of this world hath blinded the minds of them which believe not, lest the light of the glorious gospel of Christ, who is the image of God, should shine unto them.

2 CORINTHIANS 4:3–4

But we see Jesus, who was made a little lower than the angels for the suffering of death, crowned with glory and honour; that he by the grace of God should taste death for every man. . .that through death he might destroy him that had the power of death, that is, the devil; And deliver them who through fear of death were all their lifetime subject to bondage.

HEBREWS 2:9, 14–15

Put on the whole armour of God, that ye may be able to stand against the wiles of the devil.

EPHESIANS 6:11

Satan himself masquerades as an angel of light.

2 CORINTHIANS 11:14 NIV

And the great dragon was cast out, that old serpent, called the Devil, and Satan, which deceiveth the whole world: he was cast out into the earth, and his angels were cast out with him. And I heard a loud voice saying in heaven, Now is come salvation, and strength, and the kingdom of our God, and the power of his Christ: for the accuser of our brethren is cast down, which accused them before our God day and night. And they overcame him by the blood of the Lamb, and by the word of their testimony; and they loved not their lives unto the death.

REVELATION 12:9–11

And the devil that deceived them was cast into the lake of fire and brimstone, where the beast and the false prophet are, and shall be tormented day and night for ever and ever.

REVELATION 20:10

Q: Do you believe that the devil exists? If not, what scriptures can you quote that back up your belief?

Self-Control

I should break your face for that, but that would not teach you of love.

COMIC BOOK VILLAIN-TURNED-HERO SLAUGHTERMAN

I may have lost my heart, but not my self-control.

FROM THE MOVIE *EMMA*

Fools give full vent to their rage, but the wise bring calm in the end.

PROVERBS 29:11 NIV

But the fruit of the Spirit is love, joy, peace, forbearance, kindness, goodness, faithfulness, gentleness and self-control. Against such things there is no law.

GALATIANS 5:22–23 NIV

For this very reason, make every effort to add to your faith goodness; and to goodness, knowledge; and to knowledge, self-control; and to self-control, perseverance; and to perseverance, godliness; and to godliness, mutual affection; and to mutual affection, love. For if you possess these qualities in increasing measure, they will keep you from being ineffective and unproductive in your knowledge of our Lord Jesus Christ.

2 PETER 1:5–8 NIV

But I keep under my body, and bring it into subjection: lest that by any means, when I have preached to others, I myself should be a castaway.

1 Corinthians 9:27

Judge me, O Lord; for I have walked in mine integrity: I have trusted also in the Lord; therefore I shall not slide. Examine me, O Lord, and prove me; try my reins and my heart.

Psalm 26:1–2

Finally, my brethren, be strong in the Lord, and in the power of his might. Put on the whole armour of God, that ye may be able to stand against the wiles of the devil. For we wrestle not against flesh and blood, but against principalities, against powers, against the rulers of the darkness of this world, against spiritual wickedness in high places.

Ephesians 6:10–12

Have nothing to do with godless myths and old wives' tales; rather, train yourself to be godly. For physical training is of some value, but godliness has value for all things, holding promise for both the present life and the life to come.

1 Timothy 4:7–8 NIV

Blessed is the man that endureth temptation: for when he is tried, he shall receive the crown of life, which the Lord hath promised to them that love him.

James 1:12

Q: In what areas of your life do you find it most difficult to exercise self-control?

Self-Image

It's natural for teens to be concerned about their looks—but BDD (body dysmorphic disorder) is a condition in which someone is constantly stressed about perceived facial and bodily flaws.

Though physical appearance is important to people, it is not God's standard for evaluation.

PAT WARREN
WEIGHED BY THE WORD

I praise you because I am fearfully and wonderfully made; your works are wonderful, I know that full well. My frame was not hidden from you when I was made in the secret place, when I was woven together in the depths of the earth. Your eyes saw my unformed body; all the days ordained for me were written in your book before one of them came to be.

PSALM 139:14–16 NIV

And God said, Let us make man in our image, after our likeness. . . . So God created man in his own image, in the image of God created he him; male and female created he them.

GENESIS 1:26–27

For we are his workmanship, created in Christ Jesus unto good works, which God hath before ordained that we should walk in them.

EPHESIANS 2:10

For the LORD shall be thy confidence, and shall keep thy foot from being taken.

PROVERBS 3:26

For those God foreknew he also predestined to be conformed to the image of his Son, that he might be the firstborn among many brothers and sisters.

ROMANS 8:29 NIV

I am the vine, ye are the branches: He that abideth in me, and I in him, the same bringeth forth much fruit: for without me ye can do nothing.

JOHN 15:5

These things have I spoken unto you, that my joy might remain in you, and that your joy might be full.

JOHN 15:11

For as he thinketh in his heart, so is he.

PROVERBS 23:7

Q: How do you think you appear to others, and how important are their opinions to your self-worth?

Self-Pity

Def.: Pity for oneself, especially exaggerated pity; a self-indulgent dwelling on one's own misfortune; an attitude in which you believe you don't deserve what happened to you.

Love works wisely and gently in a soul where he wills it, powerfully extinguishing short temper, envy, and all passions of anger and self-pity.

WALTER HILTON
TOWARD A PERFECT LOVE

My tears have been my meat day and night, while they continually say unto me, Where is thy God?

PSALM 42:3

The LORD came to him, and he said unto him, What doest thou here, Elijah? And he said, I have been very jealous for the LORD God of hosts: for the children of Israel have forsaken thy covenant, thrown down thine altars, and slain thy prophets with the sword; and I, even I only, am left; and they seek my life, to take it away.

1 KINGS 19:9–10

And Job spake, and said, Let the day perish wherein I was born, and the night in which it was said, There is a man child conceived.

JOB 3:2–3

He himself went a day's journey into the wilderness. He came to a broom bush, sat down under it and prayed that he might die. "I have had enough, LORD," he said. "Take my life; I am no better than my ancestors."

1 KINGS 19:4 NIV

And Moses said unto the LORD, O my LORD, I am not eloquent. . .but I am slow of speech, and of a slow tongue. And the LORD said unto him, Who hath made man's mouth? or who maketh the dumb, or deaf, or the seeing, or the blind? have not I the LORD? Now therefore go, and I will be with thy mouth, and teach thee what thou shalt say.

EXODUS 4:10–12

For who makes you different from anyone else? What do you have that you did not receive? And if you did receive it, why do you boast as though you did not?

1 CORINTHIANS 4:7 NIV

Ye were not redeemed with corruptible things, as silver and gold. . . But with the precious blood of Christ.

1 PETER 1:18–19

For I was envious at the foolish, when I saw the prosperity of the wicked. Verily I have cleansed my heart in vain, and washed my hands in innocency. For all the day long have I been plagued, and chastened every morning. When I thought to know this, it was too painful for me; Until I went into the sanctuary of God; then understood I their end.

PSALM 73:3, 13–14, 16–17

Q: In what circumstances are you most greatly tempted to indulge in self-pity?

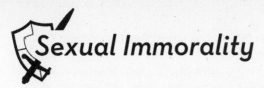
Sexual Immorality

According to a 2008 survey by Teenage Research Unlimited, about 10% of teenagers said they'd had sex by age 14, while 20% said they'd had sex between ages 15 and 16.

Many a man thinks he is buying pleasure, when he is really selling himself a slave to it.

BENJAMIN FRANKLIN

Flee from sexual immorality. All other sins a person commits are outside the body, but whoever sins sexually, sins against their own body.

1 CORINTHIANS 6:18 NIV

For this is the will of God, even your sanctification, that ye should abstain from fornication: That every one of you should know how to possess his vessel in sanctification and honour. . . . For God hath not called us unto uncleanness, but unto holiness.

1 THESSALONIANS 4:3–4, 7

Marriage should be honored by all, and the marriage bed kept pure, for God will judge the adulterer and all the sexually immoral.

HEBREWS 13:4 NIV

Ye have heard that it was said by them of old time, Thou shalt not commit adultery: But I say unto you, That whosoever looketh on a woman to lust after her hath committed adultery with her already in his heart.

MATTHEW 5:27–28

The acts of the flesh are obvious: sexual immorality, impurity and debauchery. . . and envy; drunkenness, orgies, and the like. I warn you, as I did before, that those who live like this will not inherit the kingdom of God.

GALATIANS 5:19, 21 NIV

What? know ye not that your body is the temple of the Holy Ghost which is in you, which ye have of God, and ye are not your own? For ye are bought with a price: therefore glorify God in your body, and in your spirit, which are God's.

1 CORINTHIANS 6:19–20

But since sexual immorality is occurring, each man should have sexual relations with his own wife, and each woman with her own husband. Now to the unmarried and the widows I say: It is good for them to stay unmarried, as I do. But if they cannot control themselves, they should marry, for it is better to marry than to burn with passion.

1 CORINTHIANS 7:2, 8–9 NIV

The Lord knoweth how to deliver the godly out of temptations, and to reserve the unjust unto the day of judgment to be punished.

2 PETER 2:9

No temptation has overtaken you except what is common to mankind. And God is faithful; he will not let you be tempted beyond what you can bear. But when you are tempted, he will also provide a way out so that you can endure it.

1 CORINTHIANS 10:13 NIV

Q: Do you believe that sex before marriage is "a big deal"? Why or why not?

Shame

Def.: 1. A painful emotion caused by a sense of guilt, embarrassment, unworthiness, or disgrace; 2. a strong feeling of being worthless and damaged.

God weeps over us when shame and self hatred immobilize us.

BRENNAN MANNING
THE RABBI'S HEARTBEAT

I fell upon my knees, and spread out my hands unto the LORD my God, And said, O my God, I am ashamed and blush to lift up my face to thee, my God: for our iniquities are increased over our head, and our trespass is grown up unto the heavens.

EZRA 9:5–6

But he was wounded for our transgressions, he was bruised for our iniquities. . .and with his stripes we are healed.

ISAIAH 53:5

As it is written, Behold, I lay in Sion a stumblingstone and rock of offence: and whosoever believeth on him shall not be ashamed.

ROMANS 9:33

Fear not; for thou shalt not be ashamed: neither be thou confounded; for thou shalt not be put to shame: for thou shalt forget the shame of thy youth, and shalt not remember the reproach of thy widowhood any more. For thy Maker is thine husband; the LORD of hosts is his name; and thy Redeemer the Holy One of Israel; The God of the whole earth shall he be called.

ISAIAH 54:4–5

I trust in you; do not let me be put to shame, nor let my enemies triumph over me. No one who hopes in you will ever be put to shame, but shame will come on those who are treacherous without cause.

PSALM 25:2–3 NIV

For the scripture saith, Whosoever believeth on him shall not be ashamed.

ROMANS 10:11

Q: Feeling shame can drive us to repentance, but what happens if we don't accept forgiveness?

Talents

Some have an ear for music. Some are artists. Some swim the English Channel. Some know buttons. Some know Shakespeare. Some are mothers. And some people can dance.

FROM THE MOVIE *THE CURIOUS CASE OF BENJAMIN BUTTON*

If you're not stretching yourself and your talents ask yourself why not? And then do something about it.

TED W. ENGSTROM
THE PURSUIT OF EXCELLENCE

And I was afraid, and went and hid thy talent in the earth: lo, there thou hast that is thine. His lord answered and said unto him, Thou wicked and slothful servant. . . . Take therefore the talent from him, and give it unto him which hath ten talents. For unto every one that hath shall be given, and he shall have abundance: but from him that hath not shall be taken away even that which he hath. And cast ye the unprofitable servant into outer darkness: there shall be weeping and gnashing of teeth.

MATTHEW 25:25–26, 28–30

A man's gift maketh room for him, and bringeth him before great men.

PROVERBS 18:16

For God's gifts and his call are irrevocable.

ROMANS 11:29 NIV

Having then gifts differing according to the grace that is given to us, whether prophecy, let us prophesy according to the proportion of faith; Or ministry, let us wait on our ministering: or he that teacheth, on teaching; Or he that exhorteth, on exhortation: he that giveth, let him do it with simplicity; he that ruleth, with diligence; he that sheweth mercy, with cheerfulness.

ROMANS 12:6–8

For unto whomsoever much is given, of him shall be much required: and to whom men have committed much, of him they will ask the more.

LUKE 12:48

Q: What are the main, obvious talents God has given you? What other hidden talents might you have?

Temptation

A temptation resisted is a true measure of character.

It's always easier to avoid temptation than to resist it.

RANDY ALCORN
THE PURITY PRINCIPLE

And Jesus answered and said unto him, Get thee behind me, Satan: for it is written, Thou shalt worship the Lord thy God, and him only shalt thou serve.

LUKE 4:8

There hath no temptation taken you but such as is common to man: but God is faithful, who will not suffer you to be tempted above that ye are able; but will with the temptation also make a way to escape, that ye may be able to bear it.

1 CORINTHIANS 10:13

Finally, my brethren, be strong in the Lord, and in the power of his might. Put on the whole armour of God, that ye may be able to stand against the wiles of the devil. For we wrestle not against flesh and blood, but against principalities, against powers, against the rulers of the darkness of this world, against spiritual wickedness in high places.

EPHESIANS 6:10–12

My brethren, count it all joy when ye fall into divers temptations; Knowing this, that the trying of your faith worketh patience. But let patience have her perfect work, that ye may be perfect and entire, wanting nothing.

JAMES 1:2–4

The Lord knoweth how to deliver the godly out of temptations, and to reserve the unjust unto the day of judgment to be punished.

2 PETER 2:9

Blessed is the man that endureth temptation: for when he is tried, he shall receive the crown of life, which the Lord hath promised to them that love him. Let no man say when he is tempted, I am tempted of God: for God cannot be tempted with evil, neither tempteth he any man. Then when lust hath conceived, it bringeth forth sin: and sin, when it is finished, bringeth forth death.

JAMES 1:12–13, 15

My son, if sinners entice thee, consent thou not.

PROVERBS 1:10

Watch and pray, that ye enter not into temptation: the spirit indeed is willing, but the flesh is weak.

MATTHEW 26:41

And when he was at the place, he said unto them, Pray that ye enter not into temptation.

LUKE 22:40

Because thou hast kept the word of my patience, I also will keep thee from the hour of temptation, which shall come upon all the world, to try them that dwell upon the earth.

REVELATION 3:10

For in that he himself hath suffered being tempted, he is able to succour them that are tempted.

HEBREWS 2:18

For we have not an high priest which cannot be touched with the feeling of our infirmities; but was in all points tempted like as we are, yet without sin.

HEBREWS 4:15

These things I have spoken unto you, that in me ye might have peace. In the world ye shall have tribulation: but be of good cheer; I have overcome the world.

JOHN 16:33

Q: What is your first reaction when temptation strikes suddenly? What is your second reaction?

Thankfulness

In a 2011 survey of "Recession Generation" teens 16–18, 64% are more grateful for what they have than they were in 2007; 56% now appreciate their parents' hard work more.

People had more than they needed. We had no idea what was precious and what wasn't. We threw away things people kill each other for now.

FROM THE MOVIE *THE BOOK OF ELI*

I thank my God upon every remembrance of you, always in every prayer of mine for you all making request with joy, for your fellowship in the gospel from the first day until now.

PHILIPPIANS 1:3–5

In every thing give thanks: for this is the will of God in Christ Jesus concerning you.

1 THESSALONIANS 5:18

Let us come before his presence with thanksgiving, and make a joyful noise unto him with psalms.

PSALM 95:2

Enter into his gates with thanksgiving, and into his courts with praise: be thankful unto him, and bless his name.

PSALM 100:4

O give thanks unto the LORD; call upon his name: make known his deeds among the people.

PSALM 105:1

O give thanks unto the LORD; for he is good: because his mercy endureth for ever.

PSALM 118:1

Giving thanks always for all things unto God and the Father in the name of our Lord Jesus Christ. . .

EPHESIANS 5:20

Saying, Amen: Blessing, and glory, and wisdom, and thanksgiving, and honour, and power, and might, be unto our God for ever and ever. Amen.

REVELATION 7:12

O give thanks unto the LORD; for he is good: for his mercy endureth for ever.

PSALM 136:1

Q: Are more thankful now than when you were younger? Do you express your thankfulness?

Thoughts

Often, we allow our thoughts to shape us, rather than consciously choosing to shape our thoughts.

SHELLY BEACH
THE SILENT SEDUCTION OF SELF-TALK

But those things which proceed out of the mouth come forth from the heart; and they defile the man. For out of the heart proceed evil thoughts, murders, adulteries, fornications, thefts, false witness, blasphemies.

MATTHEW 15:18–19

Set your affection on things above, not on things on the earth.

COLOSSIANS 3:2

And be not conformed to this world: but be ye transformed by the renewing of your mind, that ye may prove what is that good, and acceptable, and perfect, will of God.

ROMANS 12:2

Let this mind be in you, which was also in Christ Jesus.

PHILIPPIANS 2:5

And herein do I exercise myself, to have always a conscience void to offence toward God, and toward men.

ACTS 24:16

Finally, brethren, whatsoever things are true, whatsoever things are honest, whatsoever things are just, whatsoever things are pure, whatsoever things are lovely, whatsoever things are of good report; if there be any virtue, and if there be any praise, think on these things.

PHILIPPIANS 4:8

The wicked, through the pride of his countenance, will not seek after God: God is not in all his thoughts.

PSALM 10:4

For my thoughts are not your thoughts, neither are your ways my ways, saith the LORD.

ISAIAH 55:8

But when they shall lead you, and deliver you up, take no thought beforehand what ye shall speak, neither do ye premeditate: but whatsoever shall be given you in that hour, that speak ye: for it is not ye that speak, but the Holy Ghost.

MARK 13:11

Therefore I say unto you, Take no thought for your life, what ye shall eat, or what ye shall drink; nor yet for your body, what ye shall put on. Is not the life more than meat, and the body than raiment?

MATTHEW 6:25

The LORD knoweth the thoughts of man, that they are vanity.

PSALM 94:11

Are ye not then partial in yourselves, and are become judges of evil thoughts?

JAMES 2:4

Q: Do you believe you can control your thoughts? What steps can you take to do so today?

Trouble

In a 2011 survey, 32% of teens who drank said they did so "to forget their troubles." 24% drank to help "deal with problems at home."

I know God will not give me anything I can't handle. I just wish He didn't trust me so much.

MOTHER TERESA

The LORD also will be a refuge for the oppressed, a refuge in times of trouble.

PSALM 9:9

For in the time of trouble he shall hide me in his pavilion: in the secret of his tabernacle shall he hide me; he shall set me up upon a rock.

PSALM 27:5

I will be glad and rejoice in thy mercy: for thou hast considered my trouble; thou hast known my soul in adversities. . . . Have mercy upon me, O LORD, for I am in trouble: mine eye is consumed with grief, yea, my soul and my belly.

PSALM 31:7, 9

Cast thy burden upon the LORD, and he shall sustain thee: he shall never suffer the righteous to be moved.

PSALM 55:22

But the salvation of the righteous is of the LORD: he is their strength in the time of trouble. And the LORD shall help them, and deliver them: he shall deliver them from the wicked, and save them, because they trust in him.

PSALM 37:39–40

God is our refuge and strength, a very present help in trouble.

PSALM 46:1

The LORD is my rock, and my fortress, and my deliverer; my God, my strength, in whom I will trust; my buckler, and the horn of my salvation, and my high tower. I will call upon the LORD, who is worthy to be praised: so shall I be saved from mine enemies.

PSALM 18:2–3

Though I walk in the midst of trouble, thou wilt revive me: thou shalt stretch forth thine hand against the wrath of mine enemies, and thy right hand shall save me. The LORD will perfect that which concerneth me: thy mercy, O LORD, endureth for ever: forsake not the works of thine own hands.

PSALM 138:7–8

Blessed be God, even the Father of our Lord Jesus Christ, the Father of mercies, and the God of all comfort; Who comforteth us in all our tribulation, that we may be able to comfort them which are in any trouble, by the comfort wherewith we ourselves are comforted of God.

2 CORINTHIANS 1:3–4

The righteous is delivered out of trouble, and the wicked cometh in his stead.

PROVERBS 11:8

Peace I leave with you, my peace I give unto you: not as the world giveth, give I unto you. Let not your heart be troubled, neither let it be afraid.

JOHN 14:27

Q: How do you react when troubles come your way? How do you feel when they last?

Trust

Def.: Faith or confidence in the loyalty, veracity, reliability, integrity, and ability of a person or thing.

Things happen. Deep hurts happen. If you and I are going to walk in this trust thing, we've got to get down in under all those conditional elements until we can say this, "I just trust you."

BETH MOORE
WHO DO YOU TRUST?

Trust in the LORD with all thine heart; and lean not unto thine own understanding. In all thy ways acknowledge him, and he shall direct thy paths.

PROVERBS 3:5–6

O LORD my God, in thee do I put my trust: save me from all them that persecute me, and deliver me.

PSALM 7:1

Nay, in all these things we are more than conquerors through him that loved us.

ROMANS 8:37

Though he slay me, yet will I trust in him: but I will maintain mine own ways before him.

JOB 13:15

The God of my rock; in him will I trust: he is my shield, and the horn of my salvation, my high tower, and my refuge, my saviour; thou savest me from violence.

2 SAMUEL 22:3

Offer the sacrifices of righteousness, and put your trust in the LORD.

PSALM 4:5

Some trust in chariots, and some in horses: but we will remember the name of the LORD our God.

PSALM 20:7

They that trust in their wealth, and boast themselves in the multitude of their riches; None of them can by any means redeem his brother, nor give to God a ransom for him.

PSALM 49:6-7

Trust in the LORD, and do good; so shalt thou dwell in the land, and verily thou shalt be fed. Delight thyself also in the LORD: and he shall give thee the desires of thine heart. Commit thy way unto the LORD; trust also in him; and he shall bring it to pass.

PSALM 37:3-5

Every word of God is pure: he is a shield unto them that put their trust in him.

PROVERBS 30:5

Q: How can trusting God help you personally through difficult times?

Unpardonable Sin

Def.: The Holy Spirit testifies that Jesus is the only salvation; to determinedly reject this is to call the God's Spirit a liar, and to bring judgment on yourself.

We have no reason to expect pardon, except we seek it by faith in Christ; and that is always attended by true repentance, and followed by newness of life, by hatred of sin, and love to God.

MATTHEW HENRY

The unpardonable sin is simply defined as giving Satan the glory for work done by the Holy Spirit.

He that is not with me is against me; and he that gathereth not with me scattereth abroad. Wherefore I say unto you, All manner of sin and blasphemy shall be forgiven unto men: but the blasphemy against the Holy Ghost shall not be forgiven unto men. And whosoever speaketh a word against the Son of man, it shall be forgiven him: but whosoever speaketh against the Holy Ghost, it shall not be forgiven him, neither in this world, neither in the world to come.

MATTHEW 12:30–32

For it is impossible for those who were once enlightened, and have tasted of the heavenly gift, and were made partakers of the Holy Ghost, and have tasted the good word of God, and the powers of the world to come, if they shall fall away, to renew them again unto repentance; seeing they crucify to themselves the Son of God afresh, and put him to an open shame.

HEBREWS 6:4–6

For if after they have escaped the pollutions of the world through the knowledge of the Lord and Saviour Jesus Christ, they are again entangled therein, and overcome, the latter end is worse with them than the beginning.

2 PETER 2:20

If we deliberately keep on sinning after we have received the knowledge of the truth, no sacrifice for sins is left, but only a fearful expectation of judgment and of raging fire that will consume the enemies of God. Anyone who rejected the law of Moses died without mercy on the testimony of two or three witnesses. How much more severely do you think someone deserves to be punished who has trampled the Son of God underfoot, who has treated as an unholy thing the blood of the covenant that sanctified them, and who has insulted the Spirit of grace?

HEBREWS 10:26–29 NIV

The Lord is not slack concerning his promise, as some men count slackness; but is longsuffering to us-ward, not willing that any should perish, but that all should come to repentance.

2 PETER 3:9

Q: Many Christians have wondered whether they have committed the "unpardonable sin." If you're still concerned over your sins, do you think God will close His door to you?

War

War is one of the most calamitous consequences of evil. It is catastrophic. It is always ugly. It should never be glamorized. . . . There are times, however, when evil makes warfare absolutely necessary.

JOHN MACARTHUR
THE TRUTH WAR

From whence come wars and fightings among you? come they not hence, even of your lusts that war in your members? Ye lust, and have not: ye kill, and desire to have, and cannot obtain: ye fight and war, yet ye have not, because ye ask not. Ye ask, and receive not, because ye ask amiss, that ye may consume it upon your lusts.

JAMES 4:1–3

I urge, then, first of all, that petitions, prayers, intercession and thanksgiving be made for all people—for kings and all those in authority, that we may live peaceful and quiet lives in all godliness and holiness.

1 TIMOTHY 2:1–2 NIV

To every thing there is a season, and a time to every purpose under the heaven. . . . A time to kill, and a time to heal; a time to break down, and a time to build up. . . A time to love, and a time to hate; a time of war, and a time of peace.

ECCLESIASTES 3:1, 3, 8

Blessed are the peacemakers: for they shall be called the children of God.

MATTHEW 5:9

For rulers are not a terror to good works, but to the evil. Wilt thou then not be afraid of the power? do that which is good, and thou shalt have praise of the same.

ROMANS 13:3

Submit yourselves to every ordinance of man for the Lord's sake: whether it be to the king, as supreme; Or unto governors, as unto them that are sent by him for the punishment of evildoers, and for the praise of them that do well.

1 PETER 2:13–14

And he shall judge among the nations, and shall rebuke many people: and they shall beat their swords into plowshares, and their spears into pruninghooks: nation shall not lift up sword against nation, neither shall they learn war any more.

ISAIAH 2:4

Q: Would you say most conflicts in this world are righteous or ungodly wars? How do you know the difference?

Will of God
(How to Find, Know,
and Obey)

We sometimes discover the will of God through giving heed to the counsel of others if they are definitely committed Christians.

BILLY GRAHAM
ANSWERS TO LIFE'S PROBLEMS

We're not necessarily doubting that God will do the best for us; we are wondering how painful the best will turn out to be.

C.S. LEWIS

Commit to the LORD whatever you do, and he will establish your plans.

PROVERBS 16:3 NIV

I delight to do thy will, O my God: yea, thy law is within my heart.

PSALM 40:8

Hath the LORD as great delight in burnt offerings and sacrifices, as in obeying the voice of the LORD? Behold, to obey is better than sacrifice, and to hearken than the fat of rams.

1 SAMUEL 15:22

Thy word is a lamp unto my feet, and a light unto my path.

PSALM 119:105

I being in the way, the LORD led me.

GENESIS 24:27

Howbeit when he, the Spirit of truth, is come, he will guide you into all truth: for he shall not speak of himself; but whatsoever he shall hear, that shall he speak: and he will shew you things to come.

JOHN 16:13

For the LORD God is a sun and shield: the LORD will give grace and glory: no good thing will he withhold from them that walk uprightly.

PSALM 84:11

I will instruct thee and teach thee in the way which thou shalt go: I will guide thee with mine eye. Be ye not as the horse, or as the mule, which have no understanding: whose mouth must be held in with bit and bridle, lest they come near unto thee.

PSALM 32:8–9

Cause me to hear thy lovingkindness in the morning; for in thee do I trust: cause me to know the way wherein I should walk; for I lift up my soul unto thee.

PSALM 143:8

Thy kingdom come, Thy will be done in earth, as it is in heaven.

MATTHEW 6:10

Not every one that saith unto me, Lord, Lord, shall enter into the kingdom of heaven; but he that doeth the will of my Father which is in heaven.

MATTHEW 7:21

In every thing give thanks: for this is the will of God in Christ Jesus concerning you.

1 THESSALONIANS 5:18

Shew me thy ways, O LORD; teach me thy paths. Lead me in thy truth, and teach me: for thou art the God of my salvation; on thee do I wait all the day.

PSALM 25:4–5

If ye love me, keep my commandments. If a man love me, he will keep my words: and my Father will love him, and we will come unto him, and make our abode with him.

JOHN 14:15, 23

Q: How many different ways do you know to find God's will? Which ways do you use most often?

Wisdom

By age 18, the average American Christian teen will have watched 20-30,000 hours of television—yet will have never read the entire Bible.

There is a standard for right and wrong and a source of wisdom to know it.

JOHN TRENT
MAKING WISE LIFE CHOICES

The fear of the LORD is the beginning of knowledge: but fools despise wisdom and instruction.

PROVERBS 1:7

Blessed is the man that walketh not in the counsel of the ungodly, nor standeth in the way of sinners, nor sitteth in the seat of the scornful. But his delight is in the law of the LORD; and in his law doth he meditate day and night.

PSALM 1:1-2

Happy is the man that findeth wisdom, and the man that getteth understanding.

PROVERBS 3:13

For the LORD giveth wisdom: out of his mouth cometh knowledge and understanding.

PROVERBS 2:6

Behold, thou desirest truth in the inward parts: and in the hidden part thou shalt make me to know wisdom.

PSALM 51:6

If any of you lack wisdom, let him ask of God, that giveth to all men liberally, and upbraideth not; and it shall be given him.

JAMES 1:5

Let the word of Christ dwell in you richly in all wisdom; teaching and admonishing one another in psalms and hymns and spiritual songs, singing with grace in your hearts to the Lord.

COLOSSIANS 3:16

Q: What is the difference between mere knowledge and true wisdom?

Witnessing

% of Christian teenagers who explained their beliefs to a non-Christian:
1997—nearly two-thirds (63)
2009—less than half (45)

You know, you might think about taking Jesus Christ as your Savior instead of fooling around with all this stuff.

FROM THE MOVIE *MAJOR LEAGUE*

I was getting to where I could see the truth. Someday I'll be brave enough to speak it.

FROM THE MOVIE *THE OUTSIDERS*

But ye shall receive power, after that the Holy Ghost is come upon you: and ye shall be witnesses unto me both in Jerusalem, and in all Judaea, and in Samaria, and unto the uttermost part of the earth.

ACTS 1:8

And he said unto them, Go ye into all the world, and preach the gospel to every creature. He that believeth and is baptized shall be saved; but he that believeth not shall be damned.

MARK 16:15–16

For I am not ashamed of the gospel of Christ: for it is the power of God unto salvation to every one that believeth.

ROMANS 1:16

Go ye therefore, and teach all nations, baptizing them in the name of the Father, and of the Son, and of the Holy Ghost: Teaching them to observe all things whatsoever I have commanded you: and, lo, I am with you alway, even unto the end of the world. Amen.

MATTHEW 28:19–20

Because of the service by which you have proved yourselves, others will praise God for the obedience that accompanies your confession of the gospel of Christ, and for your generosity in sharing with them and with everyone else.

2 CORINTHIANS 9:13 NIV

For whosoever shall call upon the name of the Lord shall be saved. How then shall they call on him in whom they have not believed? and how shall they believe in him of whom they have not heard? and how shall they hear without a preacher?

ROMANS 10:13–14

Now when they saw the boldness of Peter and John, and perceived that they were unlearned and ignorant men, they marvelled; and they took knowledge of them, that they had been with Jesus.

ACTS 4:13

Do the work of an evangelist, make full proof of thy ministry.

2 TIMOTHY 4:5

But sanctify the Lord God in your hearts: and be ready always to give an answer to every man that asketh you a reason of the hope that is in you.

1 PETER 3:15

These Scriptures will help you as you share your faith in Jesus Christ with others. Commit the verses to memory so you will always be ready to give a reason for the hope that is in you.

John 3:16	Romans 6:23
John 1:12	1 John 1:9
1 John 4:10	Romans 10:9–11
John 14:6	John 3:36
Romans 3:10	Galatians 2:16
Acts 3:19	2 Corinthians 5:17
Romans 3:23	Philippians 4:3
Acts 16:31	

Q: In what ways, whether by word or by deed, has your life been a witness to someone this week?

Work

Stop going for the easy buck and start producing something with your life. Create, instead of living off the buying and selling of others.

FROM THE MOVIE *WALL STREET*

If Christ glorified God in the workshop, we also may live for God in any sphere in which He has in His providence been pleased to place us—a lesson which not a few of us need to have impressed upon our mind.

JOHN DAWSON
THE SAVIOUR IN THE WORKSHOP

The appetite of laborers works for them; their hunger drives them on.

PROVERBS 16:26 NIV

Do you see someone skilled in their work? They will serve before kings; they will not serve before officials of low rank.

PROVERBS 22:29 NIV

For even when we were with you, this we commanded you, that if any would not work, neither should he eat.

2 THESSALONIANS 3:10

But if any provide not for his own, and specially for those of his own house, he hath denied the faith, and is worse than an infidel.

1 TIMOTHY 5:8

Every man's work shall be made manifest: for the day shall declare it, because it shall be revealed by fire; and the fire shall try every man's work of what sort it is. If any man's work abide which he hath built thereupon, he shall receive a reward. If any man's work shall be burned, he shall suffer loss: but he himself shall be saved; yet so as by fire.

1 CORINTHIANS 3:13–15

And whatsoever ye do in word or deed, do all in the name of the Lord Jesus, giving thanks to God and the Father by him. And whatsoever ye do, do it heartily, as to the Lord, and not unto men; Knowing that of the Lord ye shall receive the reward of the inheritance: for ye serve the Lord Christ.

COLOSSIANS 3:17, 23–24

Q: What is your attitude toward work—homework, household chores, and working at a regular job?

Worship

We do not need bells in our church to worship God.

FROM THE MOVIE *BREAKING THE WAVES*

If we see God as He really is, and ourselves as we really are, there's only one appropriate response: to worship Him.

RANDY ALCORN
THE GRACE AND TRUTH PARADOX

For thou shalt worship no other god: for the LORD, whose name is Jealous, is a jealous God.

EXODUS 34:14

Give unto the LORD the glory due unto his name; worship the LORD in the beauty of holiness.

PSALM 29:2

Then saith Jesus unto him, Get thee hence, Satan: for it is written, Thou shalt worship the Lord thy God, and him only shalt thou serve. Then the devil leaveth him, and, behold, angels came and ministered unto him.

MATTHEW 4:10–11

O come, let us worship and bow down: let us kneel before the LORD our maker.

PSALM 95:6

Enter into his gates with thanksgiving, and into his courts with praise: be thankful unto him, and bless his name.

PSALM 100:4

But the hour cometh, and now is, when the true worshippers shall worship the Father in spirit and in truth: for the Father seeketh such to worship him. God is a Spirit: and they that worship him must worship him in spirit and in truth.

JOHN 4:23-24

O sing unto the LORD a new song: sing unto the LORD, all the earth. For the LORD is great, and greatly to be praised: he is to be feared above all gods. Honour and majesty are before him: strength and beauty are in his sanctuary. Give unto the LORD the glory due unto his name: bring an offering, and come into his courts. O worship the LORD in the beauty of holiness: fear before him, all the earth. Let the heavens rejoice, and let the earth be glad; let the sea roar, and the fulness thereof.

PSALM 96:1, 4, 6, 8-9, 11

The four and twenty elders fall down before him that sat on the throne, and worship him that liveth for ever and ever, and cast their crowns before the throne, saying, Thou art worthy, O Lord, to receive glory and honour and power: for thou hast created all things, and for thy pleasure they are and were created.

REVELATION 4:10-11

Holy, holy, holy, LORD God Almighty, which was, and is, and is to come.

REVELATION 4:8

Then I looked and heard the voice of many angels, numbering thousands upon thousands, and ten thousand times ten thousand. They encircled the throne and the living creatures and the elders. In a loud voice they were saying: "Worthy is the Lamb, who was slain, to receive power and wealth and wisdom and strength and honor and glory and praise!" Then I heard every creature in heaven and on earth and under the earth and on the sea, and all that is in them, saying: "To him who sits on the throne and to the Lamb be praise and honor and glory and power, for ever and ever!" The four living creatures said, "Amen," and the elders fell down and worshiped.

REVELATION 5:11–14 NIV

Q: Have you ever felt inspired and compelled to worship God? What caused you to feel that way?